Praise for *Bringing Your Shadow Out of the Dark*

"Robert has offered us a marvelous hands-on guide, based on decades of exploration, on opening to and transforming the shadow. This is the work of a sage and skilled teacher who knows and names, in very clear and often poetic language, the many regions of the territory and the many details and nuances crucial to working with the shadow. Savvy about the range of emotions, narratives, and difficulties that one encounters in this work, Robert gives us a powerful and comprehensive map that clarifies not only the varieties of the individual shadow, but . . . also the collective shadow, so crucial to face and transform at this time."

DONALD ROTHBERG, PHD
author of *The Engaged Spiritual Life* and
teacher at Spirit Rock Meditation Center

"This book is a game-changer, a majestic masterpiece of shadow work. Life-affirming, embracing, and evolutionary, *Bringing Your Shadow Out of the Dark* shows a true path of empowerment for humanity. Robert Augustus Masters is a ninja shadow guide who helps us to have real access to the most hidden forces compelling us in unconscious ways. Raise the bar of transformation, both personally and collectively, with this impeccable guide to navigating the most challenging aspects of being human."

SIANNA SHERMAN
internationally renowned yoga teacher

"Whether we like it or not, our unacknowledged and repressed self—our shadow—dictates much of our lives, including our actions, emotions, and reactions. In this succinct and wise guide to self-exploration, Robert Augustus Masters teaches us how to emerge from shadow—individual, generational, and cultural—into the light of awareness and freedom."

GABOR MATÉ, MD
author of *In the Realm of Hungry Ghosts:
Close Encounters with Addiction*

D1211890

"Robert Augustus Masters makes an impressive contribution to culture through his long-term study and writing on how important deep shadow work is—not only for our well-being and joy in life, but also to confront the bypassing we find so often in spiritual communities. In this book, he engages us in a vital and deep exploration of the composition and potential integration of our shadows into a life of openness, love, and true compassion."

THOMAS HÜBL
international teacher of
practical mystical competence

"Reading this book is an immersion in the darkness and apprehension of the wilderness and a redemptive return out the other side. Every page carries the authority and compassion of a man who has thoroughly done his own inner work, and who has guided countless others. You will find yourself in trustworthy hands."

ARJUNA ARDAGH
author of *Radical Brilliance*

"If you feel like something is missing in your life, that you are disconnected and stuck, then this book is here to finally bring you home to yourself. Robert Augustus Masters has quickly become my go-to resource for the dark art of shadow work, which is essential to any authentic spiritual path. It's time for this exploration for all of us, and this guide lights the path."

KELLY BROGAN, MD
holistic psychiatrist and *New York Times*
bestselling author of *A Mind of Your Own*

"Rarely has a sophisticated contemporary psychotherapist offered such a thorough inventory of the many facets and dynamics of personal and collective shadow, and the many ways we can shine light upon it . . . [A] wise, patient forgiveness and self-acceptance permeate the tone of this sharply intelligent, unflinching look at all the ways we hide what we'd rather not see as individuals, groups, and nations, especially the United States. Highly recommended."

TERRY PATTEN
author of *A New Republic of the Heart*

"Robert Augustus Masters is clearly a master of shadow identification and work. In this comprehensive book, he extends shadow identification and shadow work from the personal to the social and cultural, and he offers precise and effective means of freeing the personal and collective from the bonds of the unknown and unexpressed. Anyone who reads this book cannot avoid being confronted with the question of their personal shadow and relieved that there is a way to bring the dark forces of the unknown into the light."

HARVILLE HENDRIX, PHD
author of *Getting the Love You Want: A Guide for Couples*

"Robert Augustus Masters's timely and essential book summons us to have the urgent courage to cease our blame; cease our reactions; cease every expression of fear, ignorance, and aggression; and to reclaim our beauty and vulnerability and own our primordial shadow—learn to work with it, grow from it, love it, and resanctify it as freedom itself. I cannot recommend his book enough. . . . This utterly brilliant and stupendously courageous book should be mandatory reading for every politician, spiritual or religious leader, psychologist, and education teacher worldwide."

ALAN CLEMENTS
author of *Instinct for Freedom* and *A Future to Believe In*

"Robert Augustus Masters has done a monumental job of showing us the self-sabotage and relationship sabotage that gets normalized when we live life without real awareness of why we are feeling or 'choosing' whatever seems to be happening. The degree of care, precision, and discernment Masters brings to what we call 'inner work' makes a lot of other therapy look not so deep. . . . If you can resonate with his uncompromising embrace of the pain of being human, this book will lead you to the realness that likely put you on the path in the first place."

NANCY DREYFUS, PSYD
author of *Talk to Me Like I'm Someone You Love*

"In this brilliantly written offering, Robert Augustus Masters offers us a path to genuine change. Many authors talk about 'the shadow' without providing the tools to transform it. Masters gives us those tools, supporting and energizing us in our efforts to heal and transform. . . . Highly recommended!"

JEFF BROWN
author of *An Uncommon Bond*

"Robert Augustus Masters assumes the role of guide, providing common-sense approaches for discovering and integrating those aspects of the psyche that have been ignored, repressed, or disowned. . . . Masters also provides ways in which this expanded view of oneself can improve interactions with friends and family members. *Bringing Your Shadow Out of the Dark* will change the lives of many readers, and the change will be for the better!"

STANLEY KRIPPNER, PHD
coauthor of *Personal Mythology*

"Robert has once again invited us to mature emotionally and spiritually. *Bringing Your Shadow Out of the Dark* is a commitment to our wholeness—to overthrowing the naive notions that spiritual practice has to do with being good or that emotional maturity means foregoing feeling. With a surplus of accessible examples, he skillfully guides us through the parts of ourselves we would rather deny, and toward the freedom that comes by including all of who we are."

DIANE MUSHO HAMILTON
author of *Everything Is Workable*

"To extract the light from the essence of our ever-evolving soul requires embracing the totality of our humanity, including the shadow parts of ourselves—the parts that we don't want anyone to know about or see, yet we all embody. Dr. Masters helps us to understand . . . these shadows . . . I highly recommend this powerful and illuminating book."

SEANE CORN
yoga teacher, cofounder Off the Mat Into the World

"This is a wise, brilliant, extremely clear, and useful exploration of the shadow and will be invaluable for all seekers."

ANDREW HARVEY
author of *The Hope: A Guide to Sacred Activism*

BRINGING YOUR
SHADOW
OUT OF THE
DARK

Also by Robert Augustus Masters, PhD

To Be a Man: A Guide to True Masculine Power

Emotional Intimacy: A Comprehensive Guide
for Connecting with the Power of Your Emotions

Knowing Your Shadow: Becoming Intimate
with All That You Are (Audio)

Until Our Song Is Fully Sung: Selected Poetry, Lyrics, and Prose Poetry

Transformation Through Intimacy:
The Journey toward Awakened Monogamy

Spiritual Bypassing: When Spirituality
Disconnects Us from What Really Matters

Meeting the Dragon: Ending Our Suffering by Entering Our Pain

The Anatomy & Evolution of Anger: An Integral Exploration

Divine Dynamite: Entering Awakening's Heartland

Freedom Doesn't Mind Its Chains:
Revisioning Sex, Body, Emotion, & Spirituality

Darkness Shining Wild: An Odyssey to the Heart of Hell & Beyond:
Meditations on Sanity, Suffering, Spirituality, and Liberation

BRINGING YOUR SHADOW OUT OF THE DARK

Breaking Free from the Hidden Forces That Drive You

ROBERT AUGUSTUS MASTERS PHD

sounds true
BOULDER, COLORADO

Sounds True
Boulder, CO 80306

This book is not intended as a substitute for the medical recommendations of
physicians, mental health professionals, or other health-care providers. Rather, it is
intended to offer information to help the reader cooperate with physicians, mental
health professionals, and health-care providers in a mutual quest for optimal well-
being. We advise readers to carefully review and understand the ideas presented
and to seek the advice of a qualified professional before attempting to use them.

All client stories offered in this book are composites. No story reflects any specific
individual, and all circumstances and names have been changed to protect
identities.

Published 2018

Cover design by Jennifer Miles
Book design by Beth Skelley

Printed in Canada

Library of Congress Cataloging-in-Publication Data

Names: Masters, Robert Augustus, author.
Title: Bringing your shadow out of the dark : breaking free from the hidden
    forces that drive you / Robert Augustus Masters, PhD.
Description: Boulder, Colorado : Sounds True, [2018] | Includes
    bibliographical references.
Identifiers: LCCN 2017060753 (print) | LCCN 2018002917 (ebook) |
    ISBN 9781683641520 (ebook) | ISBN 9781683641513 (pbk.)
Subjects: LCSH: Shadow (Psychoanalysis) | Emotions. | Interpersonal relations.
Classification: LCC BF175.5.S55 (ebook) | LCC BF175.5.S55 M37 2018 (print) |
    DDC 158—dc23
LC record available at https://lccn.loc.gov/2017060753

10 9 8 7 6 5 4 3 2 1

FOR DIANE

My beloved in all things
coexplorer
of the dark and the light
walking with me
hand in hand
through the heart
of every shadowland
our shared being
my anchor and sky
our remaining days
all bonus time

CONTENTS

FOREWORD

SPIRITUAL CIRCLES have a tendency to myopically focus on love, light, and rainbows, as if our human darkness and the discomfort that rides shotgun with it is something we can avoid if only we can scare away the dark with enough crystals, sparkly new spiritual practices, transcendent meditations, chakra clearings, affirmations, and positive psychology. But what if you don't have to be afraid of your darkness? What if, as *Bringing Your Shadow Out of the Dark* edgily suggests, exploring such darkness provides a true and absolutely foundational path to authentic illumination? What if some of us even bloom in the dark?

Many of us are afraid of what we might uncover if we dare to dive into our dark sides. After all, what monsters might be hiding under the beds of our psyches? If it's true what mystics say, that we are all interconnected in Oneness, does that mean we could all have a murderer or a rapist or a cheat or a liar or a greedy materialist or a manipulative sexpot or a self-centered narcissist inside us? We wonder, "How will I navigate life if I find that I am not as righteous, pure, innocent, and certain of my integrity as I once thought I was? What will happen if I get flooded by all this darkness? Will I get lost down the rabbit hole and never come back into the light?"

Anyone who has done even a smidgen of shadow work knows that what we find when we go spelunking into the darker recesses of the inner world can evoke considerable discomfort and pain. As the veils of denial peel away, we see with ever-clearer vision how we have unwittingly harmed ourselves and, even more agonizingly, those we love. To courageously lean into this much discomfort requires a significant capacity for self-compassion and shame resilience. To willingly face and embrace the pain without devolving into masochism requires exquisite gentleness, even a sense of humor, as we realize that we are *all* flawed, that the fantasy of human perfection is only an illusion, that even those we project sainthood upon reveal evidence of shadow if we get too close.

Rather than tumbling into disillusionment and disappointment when we witness shadow in others or spiraling into shame and contraction when we come face to face with our own, why not welcome the reality of our flawed human nature with compassion, amusement, and curiosity, leaning into how adorable we are as humans, feeling a healing comfort in our shared shadow journeys, rather than settling for attacking ourselves—or others—for our inevitable human imperfection?

The kind of self-inquiry this sort of shadow work requires can cause a crippling identity crisis if the journey into the darkness isn't facilitated with great care, allowing the stripping away of everything that is not love or truth to reveal something beyond our stories of ourselves. Fortunately, in this wise, insightful, fiercely but gently incisive book, psychologist and psychospiritual teacher Robert Augustus Masters, who has painfully earned the right to teach about the shadow by fully exploring—and continuing to explore—his own dark corners, offers us a golden flashlight that allows us to go safely on an expedition into the caves of our traumas, our projections, our tendency to use our spirituality to bypass pain, and our resistance.

It can feel excruciating to face up to the unspeakable parts inside of us—the selfish parts, the abusive parts, the bullying parts, the disempowered parts, the addictive parts, the weakened child parts, the sexual predator parts, even the sociopathic or suicidal parts. To end the cycle of projecting our shame outwards, to come into right relationship with seeing what we can barely bear to see in ourselves, takes—and brings forth—heroic levels of courage. But here, in this book, you are in good hands with someone who has dared to let life humble him into someone who can deeply teach about the shadow because he has braved the wilds of his own darkness so intimately, meeting his own blind spots with the love and presence that reveals, heals, and transforms.

If you feel ready, enter gently and at your own pace into this exploration of all the crevices where our shadows can hide: our conditioning, our fear, our relationship to danger, our anger, our shame, our grief, our narcissism, our addictions, our sexuality, our spirituality, our fear of death, our resistance, our willingness to be honest and transparent, and how we relate to evil. Dr. Masters even dares to dive into the shadow of shadow work, where so many veer off track by contracting—to take but one example—the deadly "I have arrived" virus, which makes even very expertly practiced, otherwise wise spiritual leaders, self-help authors, and psychologists vulnerable to believing they are beyond shadow or don't need any more shadow work.

In addition to being expertly guided into the cracks of where shadows tend to burrow and hide out in part 1 of the book, you will also be gifted with part 2, which delivers tools, practices, and resources for bringing more light into your endarkened places so that healing and transformation can happen. Part 3 explores the essential realm of learning how to be with and work with pain, since, without a high threshold for letting pain move through you without causing too much contraction, this deep shadow work is not possible. Part 4 expands into an oh-so-overdue inquiry into collective shadow, generational wounding, and the dark corners of our cultural post-traumatic stress disorder (PTSD). Until we can face the choices we've made as a human species and the horrific consequences of those traumatizing choices, we cannot unblock that which separates us from a more spacious, loving, uniting, illuminated collective consciousness.

It may feel daunting to embark upon the journey that is this book. Most of us resist plunging headlong into what is certain to be painful self-discovery. But as someone who has been diving into my own shadow work for ten years, I can reassure you from personal experience that the rewards of no longer turning away from your pain, but leaning into it instead, are worth every cringe. Although there is no "there" there, no end to the lifetime practice of spelunking cavernous places inside our unique inner worlds, there is a loosening that begins to open you to expanded states of joy, unconditional love, and the kind of radical self-compassion that makes you capable of offering such gifts of love and care to others.

When you know you can handle even the most agonizing pain, when nothing is off limits or out of reach from the love of your own essential self, when your trauma bubbles have been pierced and deflated, when the resistance to seeing what needs to be seen and healed falls away, your heart blows open. This heart-opening translates into unspeakable joy; an unimaginable depth of intimacy in relationship with yourself, others, and the Divine; a renewed sense of purpose; heightened creativity; optimal health; sexual awakening; a loosening of mental contractures that leads to open-minded intellectual curiosity and the willingness to not have to know; and the capacity to experience a childlike yet awakened sense of awe, wonder, and playfulness as you engage vitally with synchronicity, magic, and the mysteries of life itself.

Your mission, if you choose to accept it, is to wrap yourself in a warm blanket, pour yourself a cup of tea, and comfort and compassionately hold any parts of yourself that feel afraid of what you might find as you move forward—giving yourself a sweet, nourishing bear hug, promising your resistant parts that you will only go as fast as the slowest parts feel free to go, and reassuring yourself that all that will be revealed is welcome and will be engulfed in a waterfall of so much love that healing is destined to happen. As you proceed, you will be richly rewarded with more freedom to fluidly navigate the space between the dark and the light with more—dare I say it?—enlightenment.

LISSA RANKIN, MD
New York Times bestselling author of *Mind Over Medicine*,
The Fear Cure, and *The Anatomy of a Calling*

INTRODUCTION

JESS HAS A HABIT of getting aggressively defensive when challenged about seemingly minor things. Yesterday her father questioned her about her son's schooling, and she once again reacted strongly. It's even worse with her husband; he's learned to approach her tentatively, as if expecting to be attacked and rejected. This drives her crazy.

Joe is a quintessential nice guy whose wife and boss frequently overpower him. No matter how hard he tries to please them, he ends up feeling small and diminished. His wife wants him to be more emotionally open with her; he tries, but it never seems to be enough for her. She's clearly unhappy with him, and he's desperate for things to be different.

Alan gets very stiff and uncomfortable in the presence of expressed sadness, be it his or that of others. It doesn't matter what it's over. His mother is dying, and he tries to keep the little time he spends with her as emotionally flat as possible. He hasn't cried for a long, long time.

Katherine is magnetically drawn to emotionally distant men. She knows this but can't seem to resist the pull. She's trying to get her current partner, who tends toward emotional numbness, to go to couple's counseling with her, but he refuses. She doesn't realize it yet, but she's having a relationship not so much with him as with his potential.

■

What do Jess, Joe, Alan, and Katherine have in common? They all are being driven by their shadow.

Our shadow is our internal storehouse for anything in us we've disowned or rejected, or are otherwise keeping in the dark—things such as anger, shame, empathy, grief, vulnerability, and unresolved wounding.

All of us have our own shadow, which is packed with our unique assembly of those aspects of ourselves we've learned to keep out of sight, a collection accumulated over the course of a lifetime. We learned, for reasons of survival, to deny or bury our deeper pain and core wounding. All too many of us struggle mightily to keep these matters locked away, assuming that if we do, we'll be safe, loved, and accepted, only to have them burst forth in dramatic, often upsetting ways, or rule our lives as invisible undercurrents. When our shadow is running the show, the result is often discord with others and within ourselves, with suffering and unhappiness all around, regardless of our good times.

Everyone has a shadow, but not everyone knows their shadow. And the degree to which we don't know our shadow is the degree to which it influences, controls, runs us. But when we turn toward our shadow, and explore and work with what we find there, we start to break free from the hidden forces that have been secretly controlling, driving, and binding us.

Our shadow will continue impacting all that we do until we cease distracting ourselves from it. All that's needed initially is curiosity and a willingness to look in ourselves where we may not have looked before. But make no mistake: edging into our own darkness, our unexplored territories, is an act of courage. And it's a truly vulnerable undertaking.

When Jess started exploring the shadow elements fueling her aggressive defensiveness, she found shame—specifically shame catalyzed by her parents having criticized her in her early years for being incompetent. Back then she had unknowingly found escape from her shame by letting it shift into aggression, to whatever degree. To break free from this old pattern, she needs to not only directly meet her shame but also explore its roots.

Joe's father dominated him as a child; speaking back or otherwise standing up for himself had been dangerous, and so it had been safer to make no show of power. Joe's power is still disowned, "safely" lodged in his shadow. Working with his shadow will mean not only reclaiming his power but also learning to feel safe expressing it.

When Alan became aware of his shadow, he came across an enormous amount of sadness and grief. His childhood household was one of withheld or frozen emotion; any show of sadness was deemed unseemly. As he works with his shadow, his tears, both from long ago and today, start to surface. He's learning to welcome such expression and to connect with the little boy within himself—a child who still is trying to not upset the parents who met any show of sadness with a withdrawal of affection.

Katherine discovers in her shadow the root of her attraction to emotionally unavailable men: her childhood aching to have her emotionally numb father connect with her. Her work is to bring the little girl in her out of the dark and to connect with her, rather than just fusing with her (as she's been doing in her pursuit of men through whom she can act out her childhood wounding).

■

When we first start seeing what's in our shadow, we may get discouraged. There's some uncomfortable and unflattering stuff in there, and it's not about to go away just because we've spotted it. We can recoil from the dark messiness of our shadow, or we can meet it and start cleaning it up—bringing our shadow out of the dark, bit by bit.

Exploring our shadow may at first be merely an intellectual exercise, but sooner or later—as we more deeply encounter what's not so comfortable in us—it becomes more than something to think about, and more than an exercise in self-improvement. This exploration becomes a portal to an experiential knowingness and deepening that affect the very foundation of our being. As daunting as this might sound, and as much courage as it may require, the rewards it offers are immense.

What are some of the benefits of bringing our shadow out of the dark?

Far more freedom from our conditioning (our ingrained programming). Working with our shadow doesn't rid us of our conditioning but rather changes how we relate to it, to the point where it ceases to run us.

A strongly enhanced capacity for intimacy and healthy relationships. The better we know our shadow, the less likely it is to sabotage or obstruct our relationships.

A fuller, more grounded and awakened sense of wholeness. Working with our shadow allows us to transform our internal divisiveness; our physical, mental, emotional, psychological, and spiritual dimensions become optimally aligned with each other.

The ability to make much better use of difficult conditions. This is largely due to a strongly reduced tendency to act out our old wounds. We stop viewing our pain as a problem. We know where our pain is coming from—and what to do with it.

More vitality. Keeping our shadow out of sight and muted consumes *lots* of energy. Exploring and working with our shadow actually takes less energy than avoiding it and keeping it suppressed.

A deepened capacity for skillful activism. Our actions, however strong, no longer arise from unexamined shadow material in us but rather from a direct, compassionate knowing of our own shadow and that of others.

This book is devoted to helping you uncover, know, and make wise use of your shadow. What I've written stems from my four decades of working as a guide in the trenches of suffering and breakthrough, and from my exploration of shadow, including my own.

I first became aware of my shadow in my midtwenties, during a devastatingly hurtful relationship breakup. All the vulnerability I'd kept out of sight since I was a young teen came pouring forth, both flooding and freeing me. The dynamic, multidimensional sense of wholeness I felt inspired me to keep going, to continue exploring my shadow. There were many detours along the way, plenty of times I found myself on my hands and knees, but I persisted and eventually found myself more at home with all that I am, more capable of deeply intimate relationship. Working with my shadow is for me no longer a practice but a wonderfully humbling and illuminating way of life, coexisting with ever-ripening love, depth, and openness to the raw Mystery of being. And shadow work is absolutely central to the therapeutic and psychospiritual work that I do with others; to leave it out would be a huge disservice to them.

The book has four parts. Part 1 is about getting acquainted with our shadow: understanding our conditioning, exploring the relationship between our shadow and our key emotions, and considering matters that are packed with their own shadow material, such as resistance, sexuality, addiction, death, and spirituality. These chapters are designed to give you a concise overview of the relationship between the shadow and particular qualities, so that you might begin to see how and to what degree such qualities might be present in your own shadow.

Part 2 is about the practice of working with our shadow. The material here includes not just ways of bringing our shadow out of the dark but also deep-diving investigations of how to work with our inner child, inner critic, and inner saboteur. All of this enables us to make the best possible use of what's in our shadow.

Part 3 focuses on how to face, feel, and work with our pain, because our pain and our shadow are so intimately connected. What's in our shadow is there because it was painful enough to warrant being pushed away, hidden out of sight, so that it didn't so obviously hurt. Thus encountering what's in our shadow means we need to face and openly feel whatever pain is associated with it. If we turn away from our pain or confine ourselves to only intellectual exploration, we won't get much out of working with our shadow. So we need to learn how to safely meet and skillfully deal with our pain.

As we get to know our own shadow, we come into contact with our shared shadow, be that in the form of our family, social group, political party, or nation. Part 4 concerns our collective shadow and its enormous relevance to us all, especially our leaders. Never has it been more crucial to recognize and name our shadow on this scale so that we can begin bringing it—and whatever trauma it contains—out of the dark. Without such work, such shared labor, humanity's future is more than bleak.

Facing and learning to work with our shadow is a much-needed undertaking—and adventure—for us all, aligning us with what truly matters, on every possible scale.

Greetings to the you who is already here, and greetings to the you who is still arriving. Both are equally welcome.

Your shadow, as always, awaits you.

PART ONE
MEETING OUR
SHADOW

1 AN INSIDE LOOK AT OUR SHADOW

OUR SHADOW is the place within each of us that contains what we don't know, don't like, or deny about ourselves. Calling it our shadow is fitting because of its lack of illumination; what it's storing is being kept in the dark, to whatever degree. Wherever we go, our shadow goes with us, whether we're aware of it or not.

Our shadow holds our unattended and not-yet-illuminated conditioning—all the programmed ways we act, think, feel, and choose without knowing why. It also contains all that we've disowned, pushed aside, or otherwise rejected in ourselves; whatever in us about which we insist, "That's not me"; whatever in us we're out of touch with or keeping out of sight, such as the roots of our unresolved wounding. Things we may find in our shadow include:

- Fear, especially in the form of core-level anxiety

- Anger, including anger that's been converted into aggression

- Shame, particularly when we associate it with humiliation and rejection

- Empathy, especially when we equate it with being too soft

- Less-than-flattering intentions, such as being "good" in order to stay in control

- Resistance, especially when our no to something is muted or muzzled

- The child in us, particularly when we're avoiding or minimizing our childhood wounding

- Our inner saboteur, featuring us playing victim to self-defeating behaviors

- The nonsexual factors driving our sexuality, such as wanting to be wanted

- Grief, especially in its raw depths and unsullied intensity

- Our bigness and beauty—the ennobling qualities we've learned to suppress

A quick way to get a sense of what our shadow contains is to identify something we don't like about ourselves, perhaps a quality we wish we didn't have and therefore tend to push away or ignore as best we can. Initially we'll probably only see the presenting surface of this quality—such as an out-of-proportion insecurity or irritability—not realizing that this is but the tip of the proverbial iceberg. However, once we realize there's more to this disliked quality of ourselves than we're seeing, we're likely going to feel more open to exploring it and its origins. And the more we explore, the more likely we are to realize that the quality we've disowned is, in fact, a quality that can be helpful to us.

For example, Terry's wife complained that whenever she was upset with him, he shut down. Terry understood that this behavior of his was a problem and wished he could stay open to her, connected to her. The trouble was, he felt vulnerable whenever his wife was unhappy with him, and feeling like this made him very uncomfortable. So he pushed away both his vulnerability and discomfort by shutting down.

Once Terry began to explore his shadow, he found there not only his vulnerability but also what he originally associated—and still associates—with being vulnerable: being humiliated. As a boy, when he was mocked and degraded by his brothers and he started to cry, he was belittled even more by them. Remembering this and emotionally connecting it to his current circumstances, through some counseling, helped him start experiencing his vulnerability not as a weakness but as a source of strength. As a result, he became able to remain emotionally connected to his wife, even when she was upset with him.

A BEGINNING PRACTICE
Bringing Your Shadow Elements More into the Open

Finish the first incomplete sentence as spontaneously as possible, out loud, and then immediately write down what you just said. Do the same for the rest of the list. Then revisit each of your responses, adding anything further that comes to you.

Something in me I often feel aversion toward is _____.

The emotion I'm least comfortable expressing is _____.

What I have a hard time admitting in an argument is _____.

What I'm most hesitant to express in a relationship is _____.

What I least want others to know about me is _____.

I don't like admitting that I am _____.

When I feel shame, what I usually do is _____.

What I most readily judge others for is _____.

I tend to give away my power when _____.

Your responses point to things that are probably in your shadow, whether partially or fully.

Don't be concerned about clarity here. What matters is that you're turning toward your shadow, accessing some curiosity about what may be in it. Looking inside is a process of ongoing discovery; treat it as such.

Relating to What's Contained in Our Shadow

In order to know our shadow, we need to learn how to skillfully relate—not just intellectually, but also emotionally, somatically, and spiritually—to the qualities and behaviors housed in it, no matter how ugly or unsavory they seem to us.

It can be helpful here to *personify* a particular element as a guest we've invited into our living room—perhaps a difficult or unpleasant guest or perhaps one we've invited in reluctantly, but a guest nonetheless—taking a seat in front of us. Our guest might be our anger, our shame, our fear, a part of our body, our aversion toward a certain class of people, our unwillingness to take responsibility in a particular area of our life—whatever we'd rather not face in ourselves, whatever we haven't faced in ourselves, whatever in us we're trying to keep out of sight.

Anne kept her anger not just at a distance but also muted. Her father was a physically abusive rageaholic, and the rest of her family were terrified of ever expressing their own anger. So they swallowed it, stuffed it down, fled from it—whatever increased their sense of safety. When Anne embraced a spiritual path as an adult, she loved the peace she found there, and on this path, anger was considered to be unspiritual and far from wholesome, which confirmed her early experiences. With her anger bound in her shadow, she struggled with others crossing her boundaries; she tried to stay sweet and nonconfrontational, never pushing back. She tended to accommodate her friends' needs far past the point of taking care of herself, and she wished she didn't always "have to" yield to their needs and demands.

Eventually Anne recognized not only that she (and her spiritual path) had confused anger with aggression and ill will, but also that her anger was mostly stored in her shadow. As she turned toward her anger for brief but meaningful periods, letting herself feel it arising and expressing it with care, she began to see through the aggression and ill will she had associated with it. She began to know her anger more deeply. Gradually her anger ceased being something to reject or keep in her shadow and became more and more of an ally, a resource, a heartfelt fiery force to harness and use for life-giving purposes (such as establishing and maintaining healthy boundaries).

Whatever in ourselves we're keeping in the dark doesn't go away just because we don't see, hear, or feel it. In fact, the more we push it away or ignore it, the stronger and more rooted it becomes, insinuating its way into our everyday life. The longer we cage an animal—especially in a dark, easy-to-forget cage—the worse it may behave once it's let out or gets out. This is not the animal's fault. The same applies to our shadow elements. The further or more forcibly we push them into the dark, the more monstrous or alien they will seem.

Again, consider anger. When it has been long suppressed, muted, muzzled, locked up in darkness, it will likely show up in far-from-healthy forms once it breaks out of its confinement. This doesn't mean that anger itself is a bad or unwholesome thing; its overcontainment and mistreatment is the problem.

Meeting and exploring our anger—or any other emotion—in a compassionately contained, well-lit space allows us to see it more clearly, deepening our capacity to express it in ways that serve our well-being and the well-being of others. There's no true escape from our shadow elements, for they are parts of us, no matter how removed from us they may seem to be.

The Relevance of Working with Our Shadow

The idea of *the shadow* has been around for a while in various forms, but it remains on the fringe of mainstream culture, as does the idea of *shadow work*. However, exploring our shadow doesn't have to be an arcane, archetypal, or otherwise too limiting or solely intellectual consideration. We need to see, feel, and know it deeply, without bypassing its visceral reality and its industrial-strength impact on our choice-making capacity and destiny. And we need to explore it not generically but in a specifically personal way.

Turning toward our shadow—however slightly—is a shift from abstraction to direct experience. It's also a shift from the comfortably familiar to the edgily unfamiliar, the unknown, the hidden forces that are driving us.

My client Mark had an affair and lied about it to his wife. She found out the full truth, and in the year following the discovery, he had been "good," behaving as impeccably as he could. His wife was grateful for this but remained uneasy. When he told me he wished she would trust him again, I responded that her mistrust wasn't based just on what he did but also on her sense that what led him to cheat on her was still in him, undercover. I saw his internal division: there was sincerity, hurt, and a subtle flatness in his left eye, but something darker and harder was emanating from his right eye. I had him face me and cover his left eye with his left hand, and then I guided him into expressing what he felt as he looked at me through his right eye: aggression and entitlement, tightly coiled but very much present.

As his right-eye feelings and expression intensified (with my guidance), the part of him that wanted to keep being sexual with other women started to emerge. I told Mark that I wanted to meet this aspect of him fully. With more direction, he became very alive and very passionate. He no longer tried to present himself as good and considerate. Instead, he let the part of him that wanted to act out have uninhibited expression, without any apology. As he did so, what also surfaced was the teenager in him who had ached to be popular and freely sexual. He was immensely relieved now that this aggressive, entitled part of himself was no longer hidden or masked with good intentions. By bringing it out into the open, he began to develop a healthy relationship to it, ceasing to lose himself in it so that it no longer could overpower him.

When his wife witnessed him taking consistently good care of this part of himself—and vulnerably admitting to her when it arose instead of just fusing with or dissociating from it—she started to feel safer with him. As her trust in his transparency and commitment to relating skillfully to this younger part of himself deepened, he felt even more motivated to work in depth with his shadow.

Turning toward our shadow is the significant first step of a courage-deepening, life-affirming adventure that asks much from us and gives back more than can be imagined. Working sincerely and in depth with our shadow is a powerfully liberating labor, affecting every area of our life, furthering our capacity to become intimate with everything—everything!—that we are. Nothing gets stranded in the dark. Nothing gets left out.

The more that we ignore our shadow, both personally and collectively, the more it dominates and *operates* us, with disastrous consequences. Our increasingly perilous times call for us to wake up to our shadow, to face and know our shadow very well, to work with it in enough depth so that it can no longer run us. Staying oblivious to our shadow, as is especially common in political and corporate arenas, simply reinforces our dysfunction, regardless of our achievements.

Knowing our shadow and working with it in depth can't be sideline pursuits; they are necessary practices if we are to really unchain ourselves from our conditioning and embody a life in which our differences only deepen our shared humanity. Bringing our shadow elements out of the dark and working with them may seem optional at first, but eventually doing so becomes—if we wholeheartedly give ourselves to it—not only a foundational invitation but also a sacred demand, a necessary journey packed with uncommonly deep healing and awakening.

We must approach, meet, and work with our shadow if we are to live a more liberated and truly responsible life in which awareness, love, and integrity function as one. It takes courage to face our shadow and work with it, but the very act of doing so deepens our courage.

The more that we explore our shadow, the more easily we step into the adventure of bringing all that we are—high and low, dark and light, soft and hard—into the circle of our being, giving our internal diversity the shared ground of our heart and essential presence. Bringing the contents of our shadow out of the dark so we can work with them *is* a risk because of the potential changes it will catalyze, but not working with them is a much greater risk, personally and collectively.

Let's not leave our shadow unexplored and unknown. To meet and illuminate it, to relate to it skillfully, to make wise use of it, is a great gift to all of us. Given the state of the world, perhaps the most relevant practice we can do is work in depth with our shadow, whatever the scale.

2 OUR CONDITIONING

OUR CONDITIONING is how we're each uniquely programmed to behave, think, feel, and choose. Our default ways of acting—behaviors we automatically or unquestioningly activate—together express our conditioning. These go-to behavioral patterns are wired into us by the impact of past events.

Our shadow is *packed* with the conditioning we haven't examined or sufficiently faced and that we're allowing to continue unchecked—a Pandora's box bulging at the seams, the lid only held in place by the strength of our ignorance of its contents. We can't leave our conditioning uninvestigated if we are to truly know ourselves.

All of us have conditioning, but most of us don't really know our own conditioning very well. Furthermore, we may be averse to exploring it, except perhaps intellectually, being spellbound by such notions as "It's all in the past" or "What's done is done." Though we may think we're done with our past, our past isn't necessarily done with us—and it won't be until we recognize its impact on us and begin the work of not letting ourselves be run by it, of bringing it out of our shadow.

How Our Conditioning Forms

Contrary to much of popular thought, we aren't born as blank slates; even at birth, we come already equipped with filters-to-be for our experience. At first we may only react through the filter of our appetite, interacting with life in a largely reflexive way. But even in very early infancy, something deeper, something not confined to genetic programming, may shine through the cracks, awake and vividly present. Hormonal input, already-determined behavioral leanings, genetic presets—all play their part in fleshing out our non-environmental conditioning. So much is ready to be set in motion from the moment of our birth, and we aren't in a position to do anything about it, any more than a baby lion can change its mind and become a baby seal.

Nongenetic—that is, environmental—programming makes its entrance very early and has great influence on us, given that we're in no position to resist. Environmental factors exert their own conditioning pressures. The social rules of our family and culture, as well as the directions dictated by our parents' unresolved wounding, intrude.

I remember my father—once again—roaring at me. I was five and terrified, unable to hold back my tears. He snapped, "Stop crying or I'll give you something to cry about!" I knew very well from experience that he meant whipping out his belt or the ironing cord and repeatedly bringing this down on my outstretched hands and wrists, but I couldn't stop crying. This scene was horribly familiar to me, like a recurring nightmare from which there is no escape. Even when my father wasn't angry, I got the feeling he didn't like me, didn't want me, that he thought of me an unwelcome outsider. Any anger I had toward him had to be shoved out of sight, into my shadow. Not that I knew this at the time, but it was a matter of pure survival, dictated by my fear, my sense of danger. My environment, in the person of my father, was conditioning me to redirect or suppress my anger, and to treat my vulnerability as a liability.

By the time we have—or are—a conventional self (perhaps initially marked by the recognition that it's us we're seeing in a mirror), we're already implanted with various shoulds, directives, behavioral expectations, and so on. Our deepest qualities might still peek out through this conventional self now and then, but it inevitably takes up more and more space, pushing the rest of us into the background, into our shadow, fully or partially. Our incoming conditioning—even when delivered with the best of intentions—invades us with mycelial ambition, spreading through us not just physically but also energetically and psychologically, taking root in us, its branding more than skin-deep.

As a boy, I hated my father, hated my servility before him; I hated my smallness, my skinny child's body, my trembling voice. His shaming of me soon turned into my shaming of myself. In our drama of bullied and bully, I longed to be the impossible-to-shame hero before whom the bully couldn't help but flee, the hero whom the audience couldn't help but applaud, the hero who'd rescue my downtrodden mother from my tyrant father. This fantasy, reinforced by my comic-book heroes' steely bravery, kept me from being fully crushed. The hurt fueling such fantasy became increasingly housed in my shadow, so that I became cut off from my heart.

As I continued to be overpowered, beaten down, and shamed, my sensitivity morphed into extreme shyness and self-loathing. My mother's refusal to stop my father from shaming me only underscored my sense of worthlessness. At the same time, my aggression toward him was festering, hidden and amplified by my fantasies of being in a position where no one could overpower me. The seeds of my armoring sprouted. My shadow, of which I had no awareness, housed not just my hate of my father but also much of my vulnerability, empathy, and softness, since such qualities obstructed the hardness I sought.

As our conditioning establishes itself in us, it so dominates our psychological and emotional landscape that we normalize it. One result of this is that our core self, our essential individuality, may become alien or *lost* to us. Such is the trance we're in until we begin to awaken to our actual condition.

Shifting Out of Automatic

To live with our conditioning unquestioned and unseen is a kind of imprisonment, commonly masquerading as the "normal" human condition. Though we may intuit, at least to some degree, that we're trapped, we still tend to invest a lot of energy in seeking effective distractions from this sense of imprisonment, perhaps visualizing freedom as a more comfortable place, without seeing that this apparent freedom actually may be just another kind of prison. Getting out, breaking out, isn't just a matter of awakening but also of growing up, standing up for what truly matters, taking responsibility for what we're doing with our conditioning.

When we don't recognize our conditioning for what it is, we're operating on automatic; we may think we're free, making our own choices, but we're actually not, for our conditioning is calling the shots, making the choices for us. If we're *identified*, or fused, with our conditioning, we'll assume that *we* are making the choices.

When our conditioning has its way with us, we're in the dark. The lights may be on but *we* don't really see, because our conditioning is looking through our eyes.

This may sound like some sort of science-fictional scenario, but it's simply the common condition of all too many of us. It's a possession drama, featuring us being possessed by our conditioning. The more we deny the reality of our default doings and mechanicalness, our submission to implanted behavioral imperatives, the more deeply entrenched we'll be in our shadowlands.

So often we say of another's behavior, "That's just Chris being Chris" or "That's just the way Chris is," as if what they're doing can't be helped, as if they have an unbreakable mineral deposit in their psyche—as if there's no conditioning, no shadow. But conditioning is inevitable. And as soon as it takes hold, shadow is there. This divides us: there's what we are, and there's what we're supposed to be, what we could be, what we're trying to be, what we're falling short of being.

When we were young children, we acted out this dividedness in our play, giving unselfconscious, straightforward voice to the various pulls in us, including the "bad" ones. We absorbed ourselves in the back-and-forth dramatics of such self-fragmentation. Then as we got older, we internalized this dividedness, pushing away the less socially acceptable parts, seeing them in others but not in ourselves, unknowingly housing them in our developing shadow. When we acted out some of our shadow material—that is, some of our unfaced conditioning—we may have declared, "That's not me!" or "I don't know what got into me."

But something *did* get into us, way into us, playing a key part in generating our sense of self: our conditioning. Those aspects of our conditioning that we pushed the farthest away from everyday consciousness, into the back corners of our shadow, are the very aspects whose unchecked emergence makes us feel as though we're little more than a helpless host for, and victim of, negative or unhealthy behavior.

When I left home, I vowed I'd never be like my father. Where he was conservative, I was radical. Where he was prudish, I was openly sexual. Where he was rational, I was irrational. Where he was tight, I was loose. Where he was puritanical, I was hedonistic. Where he was, I wasn't. Or so I thought. What was in my shadow was my investment in defining myself in opposition to him. I didn't see that this way of defining myself bound me to my father just as effectively as would have slavish imitation of him. I was still trying to best him, trying to prove my superiority over him. His long-ago vision of me stained my thoughts and feelings; his stride branded my footsteps, no matter how tall I walked. Underneath it all was the little boy in me trying to get his love, his attention, his interest.

As a young adult, I realized none of this. I was emotionally shut down. I was ultracompetitive. I was estranged from my core of being. I was putting as much distance as possible between me and my shame, and aggression was my go-to strategy for doing so. I was so lost I didn't know I was lost.

Reactivity Unmasked

Our shadow-bound conditioning shows itself most often through reactivity. When we're reactive, we're automatically reverting to and acting out conditioned behavior, usually in ways that are emotionally disproportionate to what's warranted in a given situation.

Reactivity is the knee-jerk dramatization of activated shadow material. Self-justifying and far from self-reflective, reactivity features a very predictable take on what's going on, which we proceed with even if we know better.

The signs of reactivity include:

An exaggerated attachment to being right. If someone points out this attachment to us when we're being reactive, it usually only amplifies our righteousness.

Emotional distortion and/or overload. More often than not, this behavior gets quite melodramatic. We may use emotional intensity to back up what we're doing.

Using the same words and ideas from previous times we've been triggered. It's as if we're on stage saying our lines as dictated by the same old script. We're acting and re-acting, even when we know we're doing so.

A lack of—or an opposition to—self-reflection. The refusal to step back, even just a bit, from what's happening fuels the continuation of our reactivity.

A loss of connection with whomever we're upset with. Our heart closes.

A loss of connection with our core. We're immersed instead in our reactivity.

Here's an example of how to skillfully—and nonreactively—handle reactivity. Imagine you're embroiled in a reactive argument with your partner or a close friend. You're dangerously close to making a decision about your relationship to them that you vaguely sense you'll later regret, but damned if you're going to hold back now! After all, don't you have a right to be heard?

Things are getting very edgy. Then, rather than continuing your righteous, over-the-top dramatics, you admit to yourself that you're being reactive. Period. You step back just a bit from all the sound, fury, and pressure to make a decision about your relationship with this person. You're still churning inside, but the context has shifted. You're starting to make some space for the reactive you instead of continuing to identify with it. There's no dissociation here—just a dose of healthy separation, some degree of holding space for yourself, perhaps even some trace of emerging care for the other person.

On the outside, you're slowing down and ceasing to attack the other, saying nothing more than what you're feeling, without blaming the other for this. You're starting to allow yourself to be vulnerable with the other. *You're interrupting your own reactivity.*

Your intuition begins to shine through all the fuss. You start to realize that, while you were being reactive, your voice sounded much like it did when you were seven or eight years old. The same desperation, the same drivenness, the same cadence. You were hurting considerably then and trying to keep your hurt out of sight, because earlier times of expressing it had been met with parental rejection and shaming.

You're still on shaky ground, though, and could still easily slip back into your reactive stance. Just one more shaming or otherwise unskillful comment from the other could do the trick. So you soften your jaw and belly, bend your knees slightly, and take five deep breaths, making sure that you count each breath on the exhale. You know from previous experience that these somatic adjustments will help settle you; they are your go-to calming responses for stressful moments.

As the out-front reality of your reactivity is now in clear sight, you feel shame. Some of this is a beneficial shame, activating your conscience, letting you know that you crossed a line with the other and that a genuine expression of remorse is fitting. You say you're sorry, with obvious vulnerability. Sadness surfaces in you. You don't make excuses for your reactivity. Instead, you make your connection with the other more important than being right.

And a very different kind of shame also arises, one that's far from beneficial. This shame activates not your conscience but your inner critic (heartlessly negative self-appraisal). It's aimed not at your behavior but at your very being, taking the form of self-flagellation for having slipped—a self-condemnation that, if allowed to run free, mires you in guilt and keeps you from reconnecting with the other.

You acknowledge the presence of this toxic shame, saying to yourself that your inner critic is present. It's not nearly as strong as it usually is, fading quickly as you name it. You choose to address it in depth later on, outside of the argument you were just having, as part of your ongoing shadow work. Reconnecting with the other is a priority now, and it's happening, bringing relief and gratitude to you both.

■

Waking up from the illusion that we freely make our own choices—that our past, our family, our environment can't control or direct our choice-making capacity—marks a potentially enormous turning point for us. I say "potentially" because it's easy not to act on such an awakening, to slip back into the waking sleep commonly known as everyday reality. Facing our conditioning and its roots is a heroic journey, asking much of us and bringing with it a sense of increased responsibility, for once we recognize what we're up to, we no longer can so easily play victim to our default inclinations.

We need to do more than just become aware of our conditioning; we also need to develop and deepen our ability to work with it. This means feeling into its roots, seeing our charge with and attachment to its various aspects, and learning to stand apart from it when it arises and take actions other than what we're accustomed to. Then we need to keep our eyes open and be ready to shift direction with minimal delay, so as to not let our automatic or go-to behavioral tendencies run us. All of this takes some doing, some serious resolve—hence the word *work*.

When we recognize an aspect of our conditioning and have done enough work to be able to stop it from possessing us, we still may find ourselves letting it take us over (as when we stay reactive or behave badly). At such times, our shadow is still very much present—not as that particular aspect of our conditioning but as *our resistance* to handling it the way we've learned to. Having that resistance in our shadow, out of sight or mostly out of sight, gives us the green light to act—including melodramatically!—as if we can't help but be taken over by our reactivity or unhealthy behavior. But once we see our resistance, bring some compassionate light to it, and explore its origins, we increase the odds of being able to skillfully work with our conditioning. (Chapter 14 will explore resistance in more detail.)

Conditioning is a given. What we do with it is not.

3 OUR VIEW OF DESTINY

DESTINY IS FREQUENTLY taken to mean a predetermined future, a happening that inevitably and necessarily will occur, orchestrated by forces beyond us. As such, it's something that we don't make but are drawn toward and into, as if by a hidden power. When we say that something is or was "meant to be" (or is "in the stars"), we're talking about destiny in this sense, whatever the scale or context. From this viewpoint, we might ask, "What's my destiny?" or "What am I destined for?"

There are four perspectives from which these questions can be asked. Looking into them tells us much about to what degree we've met our shadow and also gives us clues about what our shadow contains.

The perspective of an overly dependent self. From this viewpoint, we're pawns of forces far beyond our control that shape us according to whatever our destiny is supposed to be. If we don't reach our destiny, it's because of some fault in us or because of opposing forces over which we have no control.

Our position here is that of a child obediently facing an all-powerful parent. *There's no awareness of shadow here.*

The perspective of an overly independent self. Here we're a clearly autonomous figure forging our own path. From this perspective, the choices we make create our destiny, but the possibility that such choices are themselves largely predetermined by our conditioning isn't considered.

The position we take here is primarily one of overdone independence. Our orientation is that of an adolescent or young adult challenging parental authority. *If there's awareness of shadow here, it's minimal.*

The perspective of an interdependent self. In this approach, we view ourselves as both shaping our destiny and being shaped by it. We sense the complex mix of factors that generates our sense of self and the directions we take, recognizing our part in our destiny, our capacity to make choices that change our course. (We also recognize that this very choice-making capacity may itself be largely determined by forces over which we had or have no control.)

Our position here is basically one of interdependence—but not codependence. Our orientation is that of a grown-up relating skillfully to parental authority, both internally and externally. *There's significant awareness of shadow here.*

The perspective of an integrated self. Here, the mature forms of dependence, independence, and interdependence work in unison, making for a sense of destiny that's far less fixed, being fluidly aligned with essential necessity—to the point of *no longer associating freedom with having to have a choice.*

Our position here is primarily integral; our orientation is that of a grown-up significantly awakened to their true nature while being committed to cultivating intimacy with all that they are. *Here there's not only thorough awareness of shadow but also active participation in shadow work.*

Where does shadow show up in these perspectives of self? Pretty much everywhere.

For the overly dependent self, independence is in the shadows, along with our personal power and perhaps also a sense of entitlement regarding being taken care of by whatever "made" our destiny in the first place. This perspective may be articulated through such statements as "The Universe will provide" or "It's God's will." Destiny here is preset. Whatever might liberate us from our conceptual straitjacket is holed up in our shadow, in close conjunction with our resistance to examining our attachment to our beliefs about destiny. Here, we're needy.

For the overly independent self, dependence is in the shadows, along with the bare vulnerability of taking oneself to be a solo agent in the face of overwhelmingly vast and mysterious forces. Here we cling not to our wanting to be taken care of but to our separateness, associating going beyond it with danger, with losing our sense of self. Destiny here isn't preset. Also, our shadow here is packed with many of the very needs upon which we depend, so we're outwardly not only far from needy but we're also in varying degrees of denial of those needs that make us feel especially vulnerable and, yes, dependent.

The interdependent self's shadow is less obvious. Dependence and independence aren't rejected or hidden away, being viewed not as opposites but as coexisting, complementary positions, both with an essential part to play in the arising of interdependence and a healthy we-space. Our shadow here contains two main parts: (1) the conditioning that keeps our choice-making an automatic rather than a conscious process, and (2) the tendency to make relationship (and community) too much of a priority so that individual needs get insufficient attention.

In healthy interdependence, we're neither needy nor need-denying. We have a well-balanced orientation toward need, viewing it in both relational and individual contexts. Destiny here is both preset and not preset.

Dependent, independent, interdependent—are all included in the integrated self. For this level or stage of self, destiny is *the directional outcome of our past and present in conscious interplay.*

The integrated self has unpacked and examined its shadow so thoroughly that it can make wise use of its shadow's contents. If there's unresolved shadow at this stage, it manifests as an aversion to—and perhaps also a sense of superiority to—one or more of the previous stages of selfhood. For the integrated self, destiny isn't something projected into the future but something that's lived now, as we simultaneously make our path and are made by it. In this, we more and more often don't have to have a palette of choices as we proceed, instead *letting the bare necessity of a given situation call the shots.*

A Deeper Sense of Destiny

When we say that something was destined to happen, we may be sensing the impact of various forces and conditions that have been set in motion by other forces and conditions, like a car speeding toward a cliff edge with not enough time to do other than fly off the cliff. We may attribute this to a combination of factors and their interplay, all arising not "for a reason" but simply because that's their nature. Or we may attribute it, to whatever degree, to some kind of divine overseeing, some kind of cosmic superagency. But in either case, we're left with a question: What's *our part*, if we have any, in such an unfolding? Were we meant to be on that corner when the approaching bus went out of control and hit us? Or were we just in the wrong place at the wrong time, without any whiff of predetermination?

The less we know our shadow, the more likely it is that we'll blame "destiny" for what happens to us. Not knowing our shadow, and what's housed in it, reduces us to little more than puppets operated by unseen forces—much of which is none other than our unfaced shadow material. From this perspective, it's a very short step to sensing ourselves being operated by a mysterious force we call "destiny" or "fate."

The less we're run by what's in our shadow, the less we'll be run by our view of destiny as something predetermined, and the more we'll view our destiny as something we both make and are made by, something that's far from immune from our choices.

There are things we can change, and there are things we can't change. A deeper sense of destiny holds both of these as well as the interplay between them. Knowing our shadow inside out makes room not only for optimal change but also for optimal skill in being with what we can't change, meaning that we develop the best possible relationship with what can't be changed.

This is a destiny worth having.

4 OUR FEAR

THE EMOTION MOST commonly associated with the popular notion of shadow is fear.

Before there was shadow work, there was "the Shadow," a crime-fighting vigilante starring in 1930s pulp novels and radio programs, probably best known for its intro, "Who knows what evil lurks in the hearts of men? The Shadow knows!" In a 1937 radio drama, the Shadow was announced to possess "the mysterious power to cloud men's minds, so that they could not see him." This entity inspired fear, but at the same time was a battler of crime, a bane of criminals. The nature of the Shadow reflected the same ambivalence we bring to our own shadow: we're both fearful of it and drawn to it, however indirectly. Not surprisingly, the Shadow worked mostly in the dark.

As young children, we might have feared the dark, imagining frightening forces and beings lurking in it, close to closing in on us. So we, more often than not, learned to fear the dark, the shadows—to fear what they might bring, what they stirred in us. At the same time, the presence and play of shadows fascinated us, giving us some fledgling sense of the dual nature of things: dark and light, obscured and clear, hidden and in plain sight.

Shadows often inspire fearfulness, however slight that might be. What's in the shadows, we might wonder, as we walk along vaguely ominous, poorly lit nighttime streets, our stride getting a little quicker. When the light gets low, we often get more alert, like our prehistoric ancestors making their way after dark, stepping more carefully, with their senses amped up. This way of moving through the dark was highly adaptive, increasing the odds of survival way back then. Who knew what might be in the shadows just up ahead?

Nowadays plenty of this heightened vigilance still persists, even when there's no threat at all, nothing to be concerned about. All too easily we can slip into being overprepared, pumped with excessive adrenaline, unnecessarily edgy and fearful. (See chapter 5 for more on our sense of danger.) Worry, anxiety, dread, self-doubt—these and other forms of fear evoke and reinforce a sense of ominous darkness, a contractedness that dims or obscures the light. When we're in the grip of fear, things often become more shadowy, more threatening and edgy, keeping us excessively vigilant—and small. The smaller we feel, the larger and more looming the objects of our fear seem to us, casting shadows and shadowy implications that surround, infiltrate, and endarken us.

Moving toward our shadow naturally brings some fear, both personal and ancestral. If this fear isn't overpowering, it can fuel our steps. And it's not just that we may have some fear of our shadow and what we may come across there, but we frequently also have fear *in* our shadow.

This fear is often not *completely* housed in our shadow. Some of it usually shows externally, manifesting in plain sight. If we're feeling anxious—projecting unpleasant possibilities into our future, mainlining negative anticipation—we may not be shaking and incoherent but we're nonetheless painfully contracted, well out of our comfort zone.

If we conceive of our fear as a wintry continent beset with black clouds and poor visibility, some of it shows and some of it—perhaps most—doesn't. Its presenting surface features a far-from-friendly topography, packed with bleak lowlands and deep crevasses, along with figures, human and otherwise, that we'd rather not approach. It's easy to forget that much of this continent is submerged, hidden from sight, being something that we can't simply navigate or walk through with our everyday consciousness. Such a vast shadowland, however forbidding, invites skillful exploration. Its dragons aren't actually blocking our path but are an essential part of our path. Our encounters with them ready us—slowly, but not too slowly—to make wise use of the treasure they're guarding.

How to Bring Your Fear Out of Your Shadow

All of the practices in part 2 can help us confront the dragons of fear as we navigate through our shadow. Here are some additional strategies.

Get to know your fear. Study it, approach it, become more curious about it, turn on the lights. Get to know it even better. Go for an inside look at it, paying close attention to all of its qualities, static and otherwise. The more familiar you are with your fear, the less the chances are of you letting it control you. For more, please read the chapter on fear in my book *Emotional Intimacy* and do the exercises described there.

Get to know its roots. The expression of your fear might be outside your shadow, but its origins, its foundational roots, may be in your shadow. You may, for example, begin with an obvious case of worrying and then drop below that to an anxiety that has been with you since you were young. Underlying that may be a survival-based panic that's anchored in an even earlier time. Spelunk your depths.

Stop shaming yourself for being afraid. Everyone has fear, whether they admit it or not. The Dalai Lama has said he sometimes feels anxious. The more we shame ourselves—and are shamed—for being afraid, the more our fear will be driven into our shadow. Fear is natural, but what we do with it may not be so natural, such as when we pathologize it.

Open your heart to the frightened child in you. Develop as much compassion as possible for the fearful you. (This compassion comes from the you who is *not* caught in fear.) Don't tell that child not to be afraid or that there's nothing to be afraid of. Instead, be caring and protective enough to hold such fearfulness the same way you would a trembling infant. Remember that as a child you needed not just love but also protection. Being a good parent to your inner child will *decentralize* your fear so that instead of it holding you, you are holding it.

Instead of giving your fear higher walls, give it bigger pastures.
Doing so expands you. This makes more room for your fear to shed
some of its constrictedness and transition into excitement, allowing
you more access to contexts other than that of fearfulness. Fear
contracts our breathing, squeezing and gripping us, as if we're stuck
in a too-small enclosure, unpleasantly walled in. Giving our fear
more room, more space, doesn't make it worse but rather spreads out
its energies, diluting its intensity and reducing the pressure.

Think of your fear as excitement in disguise. Where there's fear,
there's excitement close by. Make a hard fist, tightly balled up, and
imagine this is your fear. Then relax your hand, letting your fingers
spread wide; this is your excitement, open and available. It's the same
energy, the same adrenaline, but the context has shifted dramatically.
You weren't trying to get excited; simply relaxing your fist freed up
your energy. The fear initially is tightly held in the shadows; making
conscious contact with it allows it to begin uncurling, to let some
light in.

Keep your anger on tap. Take advantage of the fact that fear
and anger are very closely related, being basically the same
biochemically. Where fear contracts us, anger expands us, for better
or worse. In fear we either tend to flee or freeze; we often feel
paralyzed. But in anger we thrust forward, leaning into what angers
us; our energies mobilize for taking strong stands. Some anger is a
mask for fear, but plenty of anger is fearless fire, flaming through
relational deadwood and obstacles to well-being, providing a torch
that can illuminate even the darkest corners of our shadow.

Separate the content of your fear from its energy. When fear gets
into our mind, we spin out storylines that can keep us in dark places
internally, thought-cages packed with fearful ideas and expectations.
When this happens, don't think about your fear. Instead, bring your
awareness as fully as possible to your body. Sense where in your body
the energy of fear is strongest, taking note of the sensations there
and their detailing. Stay with this body awareness, sensing instead of

thinking, until you feel more stability. Soften your belly and chest, feeling how your breathing moves your entire torso, keeping some awareness on the arrival and departure of each breath.

Practice courage. Courage doesn't mean we're fearless but that we're going ahead regardless of whatever fear we're feeling. Start with small acts of courage, doing things that are a bit scary, a bit daunting. This could mean having a cold shower when you're feeling overly sluggish, or saying no to a lunch date with a friend who you know you'll find draining to be around today. Honor your everyday courage; sometimes getting out of bed asks more from us than does parachuting from a plane.

As you practice courage, more and more of your fearfulness will shift into resolve and action. Some of it may remain, keeping you on your toes. And some of it may morph into the kind of anger that helps fuel needed stands. Remember that practicing courage helps immensely in facing and entering your shadow.

For a deeply comprehensive and experiential exploration of how to work with fear, please see the chapter on fear in my book *Emotional Intimacy*.

■

If you're looking for genuine transformation, you need look no further than your fear. For in it there exists not only an abundance of trapped energy but also the very testing and challenge that we need in order to live a deeper, more authentic life.

The dragon's cave awaits. However shadowed it may be, you know where it is, and you can see it more clearly as you move toward it, step by conscious step, bringing the fearful you into your heart, with your adrenaline not so much fueling your fear as your courage and investigative excitement.

5 **OUR SENSE OF DANGER**

OUR SENSE OF DANGER may arise in seemingly far from danger-ous circumstances. It may kick in with an intensity that doesn't fit the situation at hand. This doesn't mean we're being "ridiculous," "silly," or "oversensitive"—or some other self-shaming term—but that an earlier, more deeply rooted sense of danger has been triggered and is surfacing, *energetically emerging from our shadow*, regardless of our efforts to numb it.

Such emergence takes shape in three basic ways: cognitive, emotional, and instinctual. I've put them in this order because this is how we commonly react to our sense of danger when it doesn't fit the situation: We initially try to think our way through or around it. Then soon we get more and more emotionally churned up, with little or no focus on the instinctual dimension of our sense of danger. We really do feel this over-the-top sense of danger—with our emotional state ranging from anxiety to dread—but we often may remain flailing in a maelstrom of fearfulness and corresponding thoughts. This mind-reinforced tempest keeps us from clearly attuning to the instinctual—that is, brainstem-born—base of our sense of danger. What's in our shadow here are the *roots* of our sense of danger.

It's helpful to consider the surfacing of our sense of danger—and the parallel *decreasing* of our sense of safety—as a layering of sorts. The cogni-tive layer is on the top, the instinctual on the bottom, and the emotional messily sandwiched in between.

The cognitive. Our arising sense of danger manifests here as worrisome thoughts, catastrophic notions, and related "I'm threatened" conceptual output, sometimes including at least some degree of paranoia. This basically neocortical overconcern and overload drives us toward mental hells that are as myopic as they are insidious. It's here that talk therapies (cognitive-behavioral and analytic) try to bring about effective change, using mental means to deal with something that's rooted far, far more in the nonconceptual than in the conceptual. The most effective therapies that work with our cognitive states connect them—including nonintellectually—with their emotional and instinctual dimensions.

The emotional. Here our sense of danger shows up as adrenaline-charged feeling, specifically in the form of edgy fear and/or equally edgy anger, amplified by the ways in which we're thinking about what's happening. You could call this *limbic system overload* (the limbic system being the coalition of brain structures that processes emotion). Often accompanying this feeling, at least initially, is a longing for—and often at least some degree of reaching out for—safety, as in being comforted, held, or protected by others who genuinely care about us. Emotion-centered therapies focus on this layer, at best opening the way to the roots and foundational history of our sense of danger and our core need for safety, and at worst just allowing emotional venting and discharge to obscure those roots, mistaking pruning for uprooting.

The instinctual. Here we register danger at a purely physiological and reflexive level. Becoming aware of this means dropping down to the oldest part of the brain—where our sense of danger initially registers—and illuminating the fight-flight-freeze dynamics at play therein, recalling as best we can when such a sense of danger or "emergency" first appeared in our life. Therapies that focus at this layer work deeply with the body, feeling, and pure sensation. At best they connect instinctual experiencing—or reexperiencing—with our personal history and feeling, thinking, and contextual capacities. At worst they bypass such connection-making, overfocusing on symptomatic relief.

Investigating Our Sense of Danger

If we're exploring—rather than just thinking about—our disproportionate sense of danger in a particular situation, we deliberately drop
down, as if descending a darkening spiral staircase, from cognition- to
emotion- to instinct-centered sensation. During this descent, we keep
our witnessing capacity as alive as possible, generating some sense of
significant safety along the way—a safety that helps keep us present
amid whatever is happening for us.

This descent—from neocortex to limbic system to brainstem—is
a reverse evolutionary one with regard to our brain. Creatures have
had brainstems at least since the advent of amphibians; the feeling-
processing limbic system is a much more recent development (showing
up in mammals), and the thought-processing neocortex is a *very* recent
development (showing up full-fledged in humans).

Some examples of such descent when we start to investigate our
sense of danger are:

- Worrisome thoughts → gut-churning anxiety → pure panic

- Indignant thoughts → heated anger → flat-out aggression

- Self-doubt → contracted sorrow → a flattened sense of being

The communication between levels may be poor; the transmission and
signals may be distorted. Communication between the cognitive level
and the instinctual level may be especially garbled, as if there were not
anything really going on "below," at least according to our thinking self.
Our emotional dimension, lodged in between our cognitive and instinctual dimensions, receives the signals from both above and below, and our
emotions arise in response to these salvos of communication and other
factors (such as our conditioning and current circumstances).

Our felt sense of danger's core imprint is in our brainstem, its
secondary imprint is in our limbic system, and its tertiary imprint
is in our neocortex. The brainstem sensations are interpreted
emotionally in our limbic system and conceptually in our neocortex.
Such interpretation is a very complex affair; it's usually far from

conscious and equipped with multiple filters, all of which act both on their own and in relation to the others. The only way to tease apart this complex interplay is to know our conditioning—and its filters—very well and to be emotionally literate.

The characteristic sensations of danger—strongly compelling fight-flight-freeze reactions—register in the brainstem with instant biochemical impact and reflexive action. Before there was a brainstem, this core-level reflexive capacity showed up as contractile self-preservation activity in even the most primitive organisms, including single-celled ones. When transmitted to our limbic system, these sensations get translated as basic emotions (fear, anger, disgust, and so on), which means that we're viscerally evaluating the situation in ways that are more than just pure reactivity—ways that carry the possibility of a more complex or evolved response to a given situation.

When these brainstem sensations and/or their limbic translations—our raw feelings—are transmitted to the neocortex, we can perhaps reflect on them, maybe consider them from a bit of a distance and/or regulate them. We may reduce them to food for thought, or better, make the kind of sense of them that provides a conducive framework for further exploration, in the spirit of a heroic journey to our underworlds, our shadowlands, our primal origins.

Though we may talk of feeling danger, of feeling unsafe, and so on, danger isn't a feeling per se, at least in an emotional sense. Rather, it's a *state*, a condition. Its presence registers physiologically first, automatically triggering fight-flight-freeze reactions. There can be plenty of emotion accompanying this state of sensed danger, but such arising is secondary compared to that of instinct. Complicating this state, once we've trekked upward from our brainstem, are the differences between our left and right hemispheres.

Communication between brainstem, limbic system, and neocortex can get tangled, mistranslated, short-circuited, or cut off, and the same is true of communication between our brain hemispheres. What's sorely needed here is the kind of work that increases the energetic and informational flow between the left and right hemispheres, while bringing brainstem content more clearly into consciousness. Left brain, right brain, lower brain, higher brain, hindbrain, forebrain, reptilian brain, mammalian brain—what's called for is *whole-brain* functioning, which requires clear communication between and savvy translation of all brain parts, and that equal respect and care be brought to each.

When whole-brain functioning is well underway, no part of our sense of danger remains in our shadow. It now can be worked with in ways that are far less likely to endanger us—ways that increase our sense of safety and life-giving connection with others, and bring the deepest sort of healing within reach.

The danger of not investigating our sense of danger—especially when it's out of keeping with what's actually happening—is that we leave our nervous system in fight-flight-freeze mode, thereby keeping ourselves on unnecessary alert while absorbing ourselves in compensatory activities. Unlayering, illuminating, and becoming intimate with our sense of danger is a valiant labor, absolutely central to working with our shadow elements. It brings together biology, biography, and destiny, allowing us to heal into embodied wholeness.

My client Ted had trouble sleeping. At least once or twice a week he awakened during the night with his heart pounding, feeling a deep sense of danger. There was nothing going on in his daily life that could have been triggering this. Sometimes he had nightmares, but he couldn't recall anything specific about them when he woke up, other than feeling frightened that something awful was about to happen. As we talked about his situation and his history, he told me that growing up, until he was a teen, he had shared a bedroom with his older brother. His brother had resented him since Ted was a toddler and often cruelly teased him. Sometimes late at night, his brother had held him down with a pillow or blanket over his face. Ted was powerless at such times; his whole system went into high alert and a sense of life-and-death danger flooded him. Gradually we explored this part of his history—not just cognitively, but also emotionally and somatically—and deepened his capacity to get to the heart of his fear, accessing what he'd had to suppress in himself in order to survive his brother's smothering him. This included his anger; as he reclaimed it and ceased letting its energies contract into fearfulness, he learned not only to protect the boy in him but also how to set better boundaries in his life. And his sleep was no longer disturbed by any sense of danger.

As dangerous as it might seem to explore the dark interior of our sense of danger, it's more dangerous to leave it unexplored. The fear we meet on such a journey is the fear from which we emerge. The dragon's three-storied cave awaits our entry. So too does the treasure, the pearl of in-the-bones savvy, in which cognitive, emotional, and instinctual knowing can function as one.

6 OUR ANGER

ANGER can be part of our shadow, housed there as something we deem to be dangerous or otherwise worth avoiding, or as something we deny even having. But even when our anger is out front and openly expressed, clearly not part of our shadow, we may be pushing, however unknowingly, other states—such as empathy and vulnerability—into our shadow.

Anger as Part of Our Shadow

Anger gets lots of bad press. It's widely thought to be an unwholesome or negative emotion, in both secular and spiritual contexts. All too often it gets unquestioningly associated with aggression, hostility, ill will, savagery, and irrationality. Anger, already an outcast in many circles, commonly gets driven into the extremes of sloppy expression or repressive silence. It frequently can be found doing time in our shadow, where the "bad" things in us are kept under house arrest.

There are many things that can lead to our anger being housed, in whole or in part, in our shadow. These include:

When expressing anger in our childhood was dangerous. If showing anger could further inflame an already abusive parent or sibling, we learned, for reasons of pure survival, to suppress it, to show no signs of it. Leaving this early conditioning unexplored in our adult years keeps us associating our expressed anger with danger, so that when things anger us we shut down our anger so quickly that we appear not to be angry.

When expressing anger in our childhood meant a loss of love or affection. Given how important love and affection were to us in our childhood, we learned not to show our anger. Then we carried this lesson forward into our adulthood. Now we may wonder why we keep getting into relationships with angry partners—partners who manifest the anger for both of us—until we awaken to this dynamic and reclaim *our* anger as an essential *resource* in relationship.

When we're attached to the belief that anger is a negative emotion. This belief can originate in our childhood, and it can also originate in our adult years, such as when we adopt a spiritual path that views anger negatively.

When we confuse anger with aggression. Anger doesn't attack; aggression does. Anger can be infused with compassion; aggression can't. Anger doesn't dehumanize; aggression does. Aggression is the result of anger that's been stripped of its vulnerability and heart. If we equate anger and aggression, and cause harm by being aggressive, we may think that we need to repress our anger, not seeing that the problem isn't our anger but what we tend to *do* with it—that is, turn it into aggression.

When we're convinced that anger and love can't coexist. Most of the time, anger and love don't coexist. But when, in the midst of expressing our anger at another, we bring in at least some degree of caring for them, we make possible an exchange that can serve our mutual well-being. This is what I call heart-anger. It's uncommon but does exist, and it's a kind of love, however fiery or fierce its expression might be.

When any expression of anger threatens our relationship. If we're with a partner who—because of past negative experiences with unhealthy anger—pulls away from us when we show any anger, we may try to keep all our anger in, doing our best to push it as far into our shadow as we can. What's needed here, for starters, is a mutual exploration of both partners' history with anger. The more that we bring our anger out of our shadow, and the more that we recognize the shadow elements of our anger, the more capable we are of having genuinely fulfilling relationships.

Anger needs both healthy expression and healthy containment. To tend a fire is to pay close and consistent attention to it, neither letting its heat get out of hand nor be squelched. Anger is a big emotion. It can fire us up, expand us, pump us full of energy, ready us for strong action. It can take up a lot of space in our shadow; it's not very good at staying small or contracted, and it makes enough of a fuss there to gnaw at our attention, however nice or anger-free our outward presentation of ourselves may be.

By keeping our anger in our shadow—muzzled, locked up, chained—and denying it any care and light, we only increase the odds that it will misbehave when it breaks out. The more we repress it, the more poorly it gets expressed. The answer, however, isn't to simply let loose our anger but to let it loose skillfully. We'll continue to keep our anger in our shadow until we understand and work with how we've been conditioned to handle it.

It's important to know that there's a healthy anger—an anger that doesn't shame, blame, or attack; an anger that doesn't hide our softer dimensions; an anger that, whatever the heatedness of its expression, doesn't dehumanize. Such anger has not only guts but also at least some degree of heart. Part of what helps make this kind of anger more accessible is deepening our understanding of unhealthy anger—anger that slips into hostility and mean-spiritedness; anger that's largely in the dark, regardless of how strongly or "openly" it's expressed.

Recognizing dysfunction in our anger doesn't necessarily mean that anger itself is dysfunctional. The more we bring our anger out of the shadows, the more clearly we can see it and differentiate it from what we've *done* with it. Illuminating our anger and our conditioning regarding it doesn't get rid of our anger but rather allows us to use it more wisely, so that its presence and expression benefit rather than harm us and those around us.

What May Be Occupying Our Shadow When We're Angry

When our anger isn't in our shadow, unrepressed and very much alive, we can't yet say that we have it handled; it may be aggressive, blaming, pushy, shaming, devoid of caring. *What we need to do is identify the qualities and phenomena that may be obscured or pushed into our shadow by what we're doing with our out-front anger.* These elements may include the following:

Vulnerability. Vulnerability—transparent, undefended openness—very commonly gets driven into our shadow when our anger arises. Anger is a vulnerable emotion, and if we're uncomfortable with being vulnerable or with showing vulnerability while we're angry, we'll keep our vulnerability well back in our shadow, out of sight. This hardens our heart, making it more likely that we'll turn our anger into aggression, using it as a weapon rather than as a means of cleanly but emphatically underlining something that feels important to us.

Of all the shadow elements associated with anger, vulnerability is probably the one to pay the most attention to initially, because accessing it makes us far more open to facing the other shadow elements. We can be vulnerable without being in touch with our anger, but when anger and vulnerability are together out in the open, allowed to coexist, the possibility of *compassionately expressed anger* becomes a reality.

Hurt, sadness, grief. These elements can become hidden, denied, buried, camouflaged, or reduced to only superficial consideration by the way in which we're expressing or holding our anger. Anger often—but not always—is a defense against feeling or showing our hurt. Healthy anger doesn't have to push aside or bypass hurt. Being mad and being sad can coexist, including in strongly expressed anger.

Anger can suppress grief, and it also can be a portal to it. Raging about a loss can suddenly mutate into fully expressed grief; our deep, intense anger can transform into an equally deep, intense crying.

Recognizing how we, in our anger, may have pushed our hurt, sadness, or grief into our shadow is a big step in developing our capacity for healthy anger.

Fear. When we let our anger capture or fill up the foreground, possessing us with its fiery intensity, our fear may seem nonexistent. This is different than having our fear transform into anger—as it can. We can be afraid, with our fear being our primary emotion, and at the same time get angry convincingly enough to make anger appear to be our primary emotion. When this happens, we bypass our fear, avoiding admitting that we're afraid. (This doesn't mean that anger is never a primary emotion. Sometimes it is, such as when we're using it to put an emphatic stop to something that's endangering someone close to us. At such times, we don't have time to be afraid; all our adrenaline immediately fuels our anger and our capacity to take powerful action in an instant.)

Longing. We can ache for something—love, attention, affection—and react to the absence or perceived absence of it with such anger that we appear to be only angry. When in our anger we act as if we're not aching or yearning—perhaps feeling some shame about admitting the presence of these states or qualities in us—we further estrange ourselves from that which we're longing for. Then our vulnerability and softness get pushed deep into our shadow. This doesn't mean we ought to never get angry about the lack of what we're longing for. Rather, we should allow our anger to deepen the rawness of our longing rather than distract us from it.

Shame. Perhaps our most uncomfortable emotion, shame occupies our shadow when we're caught up in unhealthy anger, meaning anger that has become aggression. When we feel shame arising in us, we commonly allow it to mutate very quickly into aggression (or emotional withdrawal), so much so that it appears that we're not feeling any shame but only aggression. When this happens, we've simply relegated our shame to the darkest recesses of our shadow, giving us the sense of having as much distance as possible from the feeling, the mortifying sensations, of our shame. When we're reactively, disproportionately angry about something, it's important to ask ourselves as soon as possible if we're feeling any shame, or if we were feeling any shame right before our anger kicked in. (See the following chapter for more on shame.)

■

The fiery intensity at the heart of anger asks not for smothering or mere discharge but for a wakeful embrace that doesn't require any dilution of passion, nor any flight from empathy, nor any muting of the essential voice in the flames.

7 OUR SHAME

SHAME is the emotion we're usually most driven to keep in our shadow. This is a testament to how excruciatingly uncomfortable shame can be.

What Shame Is and Why We're So Desperate to Avoid It

Shame is the painfully self-conscious sense of our actions—or actual self—being exposed as bad, screwed up, or otherwise defective.

Not surprisingly, shame is frequently viewed as something negative or something that simply obstructs us. But shame itself isn't necessarily negative or an impediment to our growth. What matters is how we relate to it, how we use it.

There's such a thing as healthy shame. Such shame, which is directed at *our behavior*, catalyzes our conscience. In stark contrast, unhealthy shame, which is directed at *our being*, catalyzes our inner critic, which commonly masquerades as our conscience.

Healthy shame helps empower us to take life-giving action (such as saying we're sorry from our heart and making amends), but unhealthy shame, toxic shame, disempowers us, leaving us contracted and busy beating ourselves up. In healthy shame there is no aggression, but in unhealthy shame there is.

Unfortunately, most shame is far from healthy, humiliating rather than humbling us, degrading us for not making the grade. In its mortifying grip, we don't just lose face but also heart.

When shame arises in us, we typically want to get away from it as quickly as we can. It's as if we're suddenly naked upon a brightly lit stage before a critical audience, with no curtain to shield us. Regardless of how brief that exposure may be, it can register with devastating impact, shrink-wrapping us with self-loathing. No wonder we want to dim the lights, hide our face, cover up, and relocate our shame to a darker place. Shame, for better or for worse, emphatically *deflates* us, cutting us down to size. It's the emotional hub of not looking good, not looking together, not looking competent, and who wants to put this on display?

If we manage to push our shame far enough into our shadow, *we may even forget it's there*, even as we compensate for the effect it has had on us—as when we inflate ourselves through narcissism, excessive pride, or supercompetency. Probably the most common way shame makes its presence known from within our shadow is when it catalyzes aggression or emotional withdrawal in us. Once we're busy being aggressive—toward others or ourselves—or being emotionally distant or numb, it may seem that this is all we're feeling. But the reality may be that our primary emotion at such times is shame, however hidden it might be.

When I was eight or nine, I proudly brought home my report card. It was packed with As. I showed it to my father, and without looking at me he muttered something about, "What the hell good is this when you can't even screw in a bolt straight?" I slouched beneath the crushing shame I felt at hearing these words. I'd already learned that if I couldn't master a skill, such as screwing in a bolt straight, right away, he wouldn't give me a second chance. The lesson, which he drove into me over and over, was that being successful meant being competent in skills that *he* valued, and being incompetent in such skills meant being rejected, hurt, blasted with shame. And the more shame I felt, the more I was pulled to be aggressive with others, especially with regard to besting them physically and academically. I had zero awareness of this connection between shame and aggression at the time; it was completely hidden in my shadow.

The shift from shame to aggression—shame becoming background, aggression moving to the foreground—can happen in a split second, such as when we feel shame during a disagreement with another and immediately go on the offensive. This shift separates us from the raw, vulnerable reality of our shame—and from the capacity to use it wisely. If we're cut off from our shame, how can we make good use of it?

Shame can take up a lot of space in our shadow because our aversion to feeling it firsthand and openly—*and staying with it*—is so strong. Feeling our shame *secondhand*, though, is generally okay with us; we then get to experience it with enough distance that we don't feel all that troubled by it, no matter how cringe-inducing it may be. Think about watching a comedy in which the protagonist is flooded with shame, with no escape in sight. Seeing this, we laugh even as we squirm, enjoying the bare discomfort of it in part because there's no heat on us—just a pleasurable dose of psychological and emotional catharsis. While watching such scenes, we get to project our shame and our aversion to it onto the actors, simultaneously feeling ourselves in their shame-ridden position and sitting comfortably in our living room.

Vicarious shame is central not only to comedies but also to dramas in which key figures are humiliated to enough of a degree to apparently warrant getting revenge on those who thus shame-slammed them. We may especially relish watching these dramas when our own shadow contains, among other things, the enjoyment of seeing others act out our own aggression.

One huge hazard of housing our shame in our shadow is that our innate moral sense—our conscience—and our capacity for empathy get stunted, like plants left too long in a dimly lit room. When this happens, we have a much harder time recognizing when we're hurting or dehumanizing another. We then either don't say we're sorry, or we say it without any heart, with our unacknowledged, shadow-bound intention being to keep our distance from our shame and whoever reminds us of it.

The Flight from Shame

Becoming more aware of our shame, more present to it, means bringing it out of our shadow and getting better acquainted with what usually co-arises with shame: our urge to flee from it as quickly as possible, putting as much distance as we can between us and it. There are three key ways we may try to flee from our shame.

Through aggression. When we feel ashamed of what we've done, or when we're being shamed by another, a rapid way to get away from such feeling—meaning ceasing to register the fact that we're feeling shame—is to get aggressive toward whomever or whatever stirred up our shame. Not that we necessarily do so deliberately—shifting from shame to aggression is an automatic process until we become aware of it. It is a very common go-to strategy, with many faces: outright attack, defensiveness, sarcasm, contempt, passive aggression, and so on. What occupies our shadow in these situations is not only unacknowledged shame but also empathy and vulnerability.

Through emotional disconnection. In its initial emergence, shame contracts us; it flattens and shrinks us. If we don't stay with our shame and don't have aggression on tap, we tend to let this contractedness amplify and squeeze the life out of us, transporting us not into deeper shame but into emotional disconnection, dissociation, numbness. This lack of feeling is unpleasant, but not nearly so unpleasant as the feeling of shame. We pay a price for numbness and overseparation—relational deadening being high on the list. But there's a certain safety in withdrawing from feeling, especially from the mortifying sense of exposure that characterizes shame. Here, not only are shame, empathy, and vulnerability pushed into our shadow but also our other emotions.

Through narcissism. Narcissism is me-centered individualism devoid of empathy. Where shame deflates us, narcissism grossly inflates us, pumping us up with a hugely compelling sense of entitlement. Narcissism is fundamentally a defense against shame and any "need" to feel shame. It morally stunts us.

If we grew up with a load of shame and shaming, the fantasy of being in positions where we can't be shamed might, understandably, be immensely appealing. We might entrench ourselves in such positions, never really saying we're sorry, attacking or marginalizing any who dare to question our competency, let alone try to shame us. Narcissism is all about being in and maintaining such an "unassailable" position, allowing in only those who unquestioningly support us. What's in our shadow here are shame, empathy, vulnerability, and grief.

What Else May Be Pushed Into or Hidden in Our Shadow When We're Experiencing Shame

When we're in the midst of feeling shame, what may get pushed into our shadow along with at least some of our shame? What may be hidden there? What are we no longer in touch with? Here's a list of the most common things.

Vulnerability. Shame infiltrates us in an instant, bringing our defenses down. We're then like a snail stripped of its shell—naked, soft, and suddenly so, so vulnerable. Our common reaction to this vulnerability is to quickly reassemble and refortify ourselves, to retreat into something harder, darker—not only to armor ourselves but also to have a place to hide our vulnerability and any other sign of apparent weakness. Once we become aggressive or emotionally withdrawn, we're far from vulnerability and the transparency and heart that are central to it.

Essential to working skillfully with shame is to stay vulnerable but not collapse when you're feeling it. Vulnerability may seem to be weakness, but actually it's a very valuable source of strength. Why? Because it makes more of you—especially more of your depths—available for what needs to be considered or done.

A sense of accountability. While we're feeling shame for mistreating another, we usually feel at least some responsibility for what we've done. But as soon as we cease staying with our shame, this sense of responsibility gets swept away, minimized, given little or no attention. And if we get aggressive, we may then project most or all of the accountability for what's happened onto the person whom we were mistreating only a short time ago, essentially blaming them for our actions.

Empathy. In healthy shame, we start to feel some emotional resonance with the other, however painful that might be. The more we let this resonance happen, the more we want to come clean, make amends, and so on. But if we make our discomfort with our shame more important than taking fitting action regarding the other, we just keep our empathic capacity on hold, fortifying—and perhaps also legitimizing—our emotional separateness from the other.

Our identification with our inner child. When our shame surfaces, its strongest impact internally is on the child in us. At such times, we may identify with that child to such a degree that we don't provide him or her with any protection from our inner critic. Here, our maturity and capacity for self-reflection are stuck in our shadow.

Our identification with our inner critic. When our shame surfaces, we may identify with our inner critic, speaking and thinking as though we *are* it. We shame ourselves for our childishness, incompetence, and so on, attacking our inner child with no mercy. Waking up to such identification is a big step in growing up.

Our attachment to viewing ourselves as unworthy of love and protection. We may unquestioningly believe that we're unworthy, especially when our relationships go awry, and we may also keep our attachment to this belief out of sight. Not addressing this attachment keeps us disempowered, small, stuck. We're then just like a child facing shame-infused parenting: we find a certain security in going along with the assertion that we're unworthy; devaluing ourselves becomes a survival strategy.

One of the first steps in healing this dynamic is to bring its origins out of our shadow and get *in between* our inner child and inner critic, identifying with neither while loving *and protecting* the child in us. We then neither lose ourselves in our shame nor flee it. We're present to it, holding it with a well-grounded awareness.

Staying present with our shame rather than deporting it to our shadow does far more good than letting it morph into aggression and emotional disconnection. Being present with our shame—sitting in its fire with both dignity and humility—refines the warrior in us, male or female, and deepens our capacity for compassion, vulnerability, and relational sanity and joy.

Bringing our shame, all of our shame, out of our shadow is a great gift for one and all. For in so doing we keep ourselves empathetic and accountable, and available for whatever healing or redirection is needed.

8 OUR GRIEF

MUCH OF OUR GRIEF gets shut away and muted in our shadow, housed not so far from our fear of death. Like shame, grief strips us bare. But where shame leaves us painfully self-conscious, grief leaves us painfully conscious of—and defenselessly feeling—loss, whatever the scale. Grief is heartbreak at its purest and messiest, imbued with existential vulnerability and at least some degree of agony. When grief-stricken, we're turned toward our pain, and our usual painkillers lose much of their effectiveness.

Grief is the core-level, deeply felt response to loss and in-your-face impermanence. It includes sorrow, but is more than sorrow. It doesn't just weep, but wails, keens, howls. Its sounds express a pain and devastation felt right to the marrow. But it also can be silent—thunderously and unspeakably silent. It may include wild mood swings, disorientation, spiritual revelations, and bouts of rage.

The emotionally bruised surfaces of grief may show to varying degrees, but the bulk of grief all too often remains in our shadow. Frozen grief, muted grief, strangled grief—we store so much heart-hurt and ossified sorrow out of sight so that it won't mess with our life. But what a price we pay for this!

Broken Open to What Really Matters

Grief helps make us fully human; it emotionally and spiritually grounds us in the raw reality of loss and the inevitability of endings, minus any buffers or distractions. There's pain in it, sometimes unbearable pain, but there's also an opening, however rough or ragged, to life at a fundamental level. The gifts of grief include not only this reality-unlocking openness but also a kind of brokenheartedness that has the power to greatly deepen our intimacy with each other and with life itself. Fully felt grief *connects* us all; grieving together attunes us to what really matters.

At first, it's "my" grief, intensely and understandably personal. We may go no further than this, or we may find ourselves shifting to a sense of "our" grief, as our heart breaks open to include the pain of others close to us. We may then further shift to "the" grief, as we attune to collective suffering and allow the feeling of that to penetrate and move us. This attunement, this wide-open communion, brings not just more grief but also more love, compassion, and connection, as the circle of our being expands to include everyone who has grief.

When we're in touch only with *my* grief, *our* grief and *the* grief remain in our shadow. When we're in touch only with *my* and *our* grief, *the* grief is in our shadow. And when we're connected with all three, grief is completely out in the open. The move from personal to relational to collective grief is not a strategy or practice but rather a natural outcome of surrendering to our own grief.

Grief isn't something to get over but something to get into fully. Its heartbreak isn't a malady but can be a portal to depth and communion, ripening into a grounded bareness of being that guides us into deeper, far more humane ways of living.

Unfortunately, contemporary culture is largely grief-phobic, especially regarding the uninhibited expression of grief. A few tears are usually deemed okay, so long as they're not too loud, not too messy. "Being strong" in the presence of grief—meaning keeping relatively stoic, holding things together, not letting our emotions "get the better of us"—is often held as more of a virtue than letting grief have its way with us.

The unexpressed grief that permeates our culture—and that's stored in our collective shadow—keeps us overly apart from each other. Why? Because openly expressed grief empathetically links us, sooner or later, to everyone who has grief. And we all have grief. It comes with being human. To leave it unattended isolates us, binding us in exaggerated autonomy and separateness, out of touch with the interconnectedness of all that is. In cultures that are death-denying, openly expressed grief is a no-no because it directly and deeply exposes us to death and our own mortality.

Signs that grief may be in our shadow include:

The denial of and aversion to death. Death-denying practices and grief repression go hand in hand. (See chapter 13 on our fear of death.)

A lack of empathy when faced with others' heartbreak and crises. This lack is especially noticeable with others who are very different from us.

Feeling discomfort in the presence of others' grief. There's a desire to have them emote more quietly and discreetly.

Turning away from our pain. Such avoidance can include a reliance on painkillers and tranquillizing agents, including electronic sedation.

Resisting being vulnerable. The less vulnerable we are, the more difficult it is to access our grief.

Thinking of grief as something to get over. We see grief as a problem and seek remedies for it. We may feel an aversion toward those whom we think have done enough grieving.

Feeling ashamed when we display any sorrow. We feel shame because we associate sorrow with weakness, dysfunction, or loss of power.

Emotional numbness and disconnection.

Feeling depressed when things end or significantly change. Where grief is the heart suffused with—and blown open by— loss-centered hurt, depression is the heart *flattened*.

Shifting to aggression when we feel rising sadness or shame. This shift keeps us from being vulnerable.

Denying that we have grief. It's easy to project our grief onto others, thereby distancing ourselves from our own.

■

Opening to our grief, making room for it to breathe, flow, and find fitting expression, might seem unproductive, out of keeping with our get-ahead intentions and motivations, but it's actually a profoundly productive undertaking, if only because of its capacity to deepen our shared humanity, our cross-cultural kinship.

Grief brings us into intimate contact with life's ever-arising losses and endings, providing not a solution to them but rather the capacity and space to be fully present with them—emotionally, mentally, physically, and spiritually. Grief de-numbs us, tenderizes and deepens us, rendering us more whole, more alive, more here. Choose, and keep choosing, to trust it; however rough the ride may be, it's worth taking, for the sake of one and all.

9 NARCISSISM

NARCISSISM IS ME-CENTERED individualism devoid of empathy. Its credo is "What's in it for me?" Its demand, however understated, is "See and affirm and don't question my specialness." There's no "us" for the narcissistically bound, regardless of their propaganda to the contrary; everything that's "not me" revolves around them. Left unattended, narcissism is an enormously destructive force because in our narcissism all we care about is what benefits us, regardless of the cost to others. And if we do show care to others, we only do so to profit ourselves.

Narcissism is selfishness at its ugliest; in a narcissistic mind-set, others exist only as objects to be used or manipulated for the desires of "me." This status, however, may not be a turn-off for us when we're with those who are narcissistic, because their drive to garner our admiration and our validation of their specialness may manifest as considerable charm, generosity, undivided attentiveness, and energetic magnetism, to such a degree that we don't realize they're using us. They devalue us even as they woo us.

Narcissism can be not just personal but also collective. Think of massive corporate entities, which more often than not operate as a metastasizing "me," with no morality other than "what's good for me (that is, the corporation) is what matters."

Narcissism is a cult of one. It's just as rigidly encapsulated as any cult of many. (Cults are tightly self-enclosed entities shut off to both internal dissent and external feedback.) It's extremely difficult to convince cult members that they're in a cult, no matter how accurate we may be. It's just as difficult to convince those who are narcissistic that they are indeed so.

At best, "I gotta be me" can be the cry of healthy individuation, an evolutionary "yes!" to being more fully ourselves. At worst, it can be the rallying cry of narcissism, a shout-out to being a somebody for whom standing out or being clearly special holds far too much importance. (In healthy individuation, our evolving autonomy coexists with our felt interconnectedness and empathy for others.)

What's in Our Shadow When Narcissism Is Running Us

Though narcissism is often described as a self-centered condition, it's actually centered not by our real self but by a compensatory flight from our real self, fueled by the desire to get as far as possible from any of the following:

Vulnerability. If our vulnerability surfaces enough to even get noticed, we view it as weakness or deficiency.

Unresolved wounding. There's no way we'll approach this when we're caught up in narcissism.

Empathy. Narcissism and empathy are mutually exclusive.

The capacity for being we-centered. Being "me" is fine so long as it's not marooned from "us." But in narcissism, "us" turns into a *very* distant "them," housed in the darkest recesses of our shadow.

Shame. The hidden cry here is "Don't shame me." The grail for us when we're immersed in narcissism is to be established as much as possible out of the reach of shame. The farther back shame is pushed into our shadow, the more our narcissism flourishes. *Where shame deflates us, narcissism inflates us*, pumping us up with a compelling sense of entitlement and at least some degree of grandiosity. We conceive of ourselves not as special but as *very* special.

Humility. Narcissism conflates humility with humiliation. Humility doesn't mean trying to be humble, nonprideful, or free of vanity, but rather keeping our inflationary me-centered tendencies in healthy perspective, celebrating others' successes as well as our own, and taking care not to dehumanize others. It also means *learning to expand ourselves not for imperialistic payoffs but so as to include others in the circle of our being.* Such inclusion is anathema to those infected with narcissism. What they don't see is that their aversion to including others is none other than their aversion to including all that *they* are in the circle of their being.

The capacity for relational intimacy. The narcissistically inclined don't form relationships but rather *associations*, which provide them (or have the potential to provide them) with the payoffs they crave, such as being admired or being in enough control to be relatively unscathed by the inconvenience of others' displeasure or outrage.

Decentralizing Narcissism

A little narcissism isn't a problem; most of us have a bit of it, however muted or inert it might be. All we have to do is not let it occupy a central place in us. Getting to know our own narcissistic tendencies equips us to relate more skillfully to the narcissism of others.

The potential for narcissism shows up early in life, appearing with the rise of our ego. Consider a young child who is loved by one parent and rejected by the other; the child bounces between being praised and being shamed. This child is more likely than most to become narcissistic, feeling safest or most stable when being praised or admired. Furthermore, if this child learns to distrust the incoming praise (because it does nothing to provide protection from the incoming rejection and shaming), he or she will also feel insecure, as well as have a compensatory drive to have as much control as possible (so as to minimize being rejected or shamed).

Too much praise can foster narcissism, and so can a deeply implanted sense of entitlement—especially when it coexists with a low degree or lack of empathy. Heavy shaming can also catalyze narcissism, as a compensatory strategy. When narcissism takes root, moral development gets frozen in its tracks; we may continue developing cognitively and in other ways but remain morally stunted, whatever our station in life and political status.

Instead of shaming ourselves for having narcissism, let's get more curious about it and start examining it. We can begin by illuminating our history with it and our ways of disguising it, sensing within it a child whose sense of self got seriously derailed—a child whose sense of being somebody special became far too important.

There's a deep wound in narcissism, a splitting off from care and loving connection that drives us into an exaggerated sense of somebodyness. Our work here is to bring this wound out of our shadow and compassionately contact what lies at its heart. This labor is more than a cognitive undertaking; it asks that we open ourselves to such hurt in the same way that genuinely loving and conscious parents do when one of their children has been hurt. The point is not to eliminate narcissism in ourselves—an impossible task—but to relate to it deeply enough so that its viewpoint ceases being our own.

10 ADDICTION

WHEN WE'RE ADDICTED to something, the foreground is occupied by our craving and the object of our craving. Addiction is metastasized appetite, craving gone over the edge, a compulsively consuming fixation that we harness ourselves to, minus any reins. Although we say that we have an addiction, it's more accurate to say that it has us. Our addiction owns us, runs us. When we're absorbed in addictive behavior, our capacity to interrupt or cut through it is starved, shoved into the back corners of our shadow.

Also looming large in the background is *pain*. Addiction is, fundamentally, an unskillful strategy to deal with core-level pain, be it physical, emotional, psychological, existential, or spiritual. Addiction's central promise, hugely highlighted, is that it will release us from such pain, ideally as pleasurably as possible. The greater the pleasure—or the *promise* of the pleasure—the greater the craving for it. In this craving there's considerable desperation, which carries its own pain.

So there's the pain of addiction—the pain of craving, withdrawal, relapsing, and what it does to us and those near us—and then there's the pain of what first drove us into addiction, the underlying wounding for which our addictive behavior serves as a combination "solution" and distraction. And where do we find the bare reality and roots of this wounding? In our shadow.

Is anyone totally free of addiction? Probably not. Looking down upon obvious addicts only distances us from our own addictions, allowing us to frame these behaviors as something other than addictions—especially if they are socially acceptable. Addiction isn't just something that alcoholics, junkies, and overeaters are netted by; there's addiction to power, sex, greed, conformity, nonconformity, being positive, being negative, beliefs. We can be addicted to being good, being nonattached, looking young, staying in control, pleasing certain others, padding our spiritual resumé, and so on. We can even be addicted to being addicted.

But a little addiction isn't a problem as long as we understand it and don't allow it to occupy a central place in us. Addressing addiction, then, isn't just for those who identify as "addicts"; it's for all of us, to whatever degree. And exploring our shadow is an opportunity to recognize where and how we may be addicted.

Uprooting and Outgrowing Addiction

Addressing our addiction requires many of the same skills that addressing other shadow elements does. Working with our shadow is essential to truly effective addiction therapy. It brings into the open the roots of our core-level wounding; if this wounding isn't sufficiently faced, we're more likely to relapse. This doesn't mean, however, that serious addiction can be treated solely with shadow work. Fitting practices and support from caring others, such as found in 12-step programs, are usually also necessary.

The following points about how to effectively work with addiction are in no particular order.

Bring the roots of your addiction out of your shadow. To do this, you need to get to know your conditioning from the inside; deepen your recognition of the originating factors of your behavioral tendencies. Become more intimate with how you are conditioned, how you were conditioned, and what you're doing about it. How were you wounded as a child? How did you cope then? What survival strategies did you take on, and how are these strategies still showing up today? Cast a clear and caring eye not only on your inner workings but also on your history, connecting the dots between past events and present behavior. Once you're clear about what first drove you toward your addiction, *deepen your acquaintance with it.*

Consider doing some work with an integrally inclined, emotionally literate therapist. (See chapter 2 for more on exploring your conditioning.)

Instead of treating your addiction as a thing, *personify* it. This means shifting your sense of addictiveness from a *something* that's possessed you to a character of sorts—an *inner addict*. This shift allows you to relate more easily to your addiction. It's as if you're engaging with a *somebody*, and this somebody may feel a lot like you when you first got hooked.

Get to know your inner addict. We all have an addict in us, but not so many of us have a healthy relationship to it. We may fuse with it, identify with it, look through its eyes. Or we might dissociate from it, harshly condemning ourselves for our bad habit—and then seek relief from such heavy-duty shaming through once again acting out our addiction. *Instead of caving in to or rejecting your inner addict, become intimate with it.*

When your craving arises, identify what you're feeling emotionally. Yes, you feel the pull of your addiction, but just beneath or behind this pull are the very feelings that were present when your addiction first gripped you. Name whatever emotions are there as you feel your craving, and shift your attention to these as much as you can, no matter how loud or compelling the call of your addiction may be. Feel into the raw depth of these emotions, staying with such feeling as much as you can. Notice how old you feel, what memories may be surfacing, what you're doing with these emotions, remembering what you used to do with them before you were addicted.

Resonate with the you who first felt these pre-addiction emotions. Cultivate at least some degree of intimacy with who you were before you became addicted, bringing that relationship more into the foreground. Attune to this younger you, visualize and feel this one, giving him or her the attention that you usually give to your addictive behaviors. Make that younger you—probably a child or maybe a young teen—more central, providing her or him with both care and protection. Bring that one closer, breathing her or him into your heart, your belly, your being. Your inner addict is simply a personification of the unskillful "solution" to that younger self's pain, unresolved wounding, unmet needs. Your work here is to provide a better, more life-giving solution to such pain and wounding, replacing the "taking-care-of" promise of addiction with a healthy parenting of the child/teen in you.

Recognize that unhooking from addiction doesn't mean avoiding attachment. Without attachment to others, there's no compassion—and compassion is an essential factor in facing and healing addiction. Healthy attachment doesn't contain any desperation, whereas addiction does. Such attachment may show up as a heartfelt bonding, but in addiction, bonding is replaced by bondage. The more that we understand and get to the core of our addictive tendencies, the more empathetic we'll probably become with similar tendencies in others—and such empathy makes compassion possible, both for ourselves and others.

◾

Once we recognize and work with its roots, we're on our way to freeing ourselves from our addiction. As hard as such work may be, we know that we're on track (feeling our addiction's grip on us weakening), and we simply persist, however short or stumbling our steps may be. Our shackles are loosening, our stride contains more of the essential us, and the painful roots of the addict within are no longer in our shadow, no longer binding and blinding us.

11 OUR SEXUALITY

THE SHADOW ASPECTS of sex aren't the unconventional or kinky extremes of sexuality, however dark these may be, but rather whatever psychological and emotional conditioning we've left unexamined and are allowing to direct our sexuality.

To a significant degree, sex is still in the closet, including in contemporary Western culture. It might appear that this isn't so, given how nakedly out-front sex is in our times, how graphically present, how openly talked about. But such exposure doesn't necessarily reveal sexuality's depths, inner workings, and formative factors. *A deeper disrobing is needed.* What doesn't get adequate attention and focus are the *nonsexual* aspects of our sexuality. Though they control or direct much of our sexuality from behind the scenes, they all too often get camouflaged by our actual sexual doings and remain in our shadow.

These nonsexual underpinnings include our unresolved wounding, unrequited needs, unacknowledged motivations, and the various tasks that our sexuality frequently gets saddled with, such as:

- Make me feel better

- De-stress me

- Prove that I'm wanted or desirable or special

- Distract me from my pain

- Reinforce my fantasy that my partner and I are close

- Make me feel more secure

- Console me

- Distract me from what isn't working in our relationship

- Make me feel whole

- Make me feel more powerful

- Help me feel less lonely

Plenty of our sexual drive may be coming from conditioning that has nothing to do with actual sexuality—conditioning that we commonly turn a blind eye to and thereby confine to our shadow, including when we're in the throes of sexual excitation and activity.

Sex not only can provide an arena in which to act out shadow material but can also very easily distract us from that very material. That is, sex can both express our conditioning and keep it in the dark.

Stan was at a gathering with his partner and had begun flirting erotically with a new acquaintance. He was unknowingly sexualizing a craving—which had been with him since early childhood—to feel special in another's eyes, even while acting as if all he was doing was having a good time. Hidden in his shadow was his desperate wanting to be wanted; eroticizing this yearning actually camouflaged it, wrapping him up in the compelling chemistry of sexual attraction.

His partner eventually saw what he was doing, and at home that night got angry at him. Stan's response: "You're overreacting. I didn't mean anything by it. I was just being playful. What's the big deal?" Adopting this stance (1) made it seem as if his partner was the one with the problem, and (2) kept Stan out of touch with what he was really up to in his earlier flirting.

The Eroticizing of Our Wounds

The central shadow factor directing our sexuality is the eroticizing of our unresolved wounding and insufficiently met needs. Here's how such eroticizing—which is *extremely* common—happens (excerpted from my book *To Be a Man*):

1. We get significantly hurt in our early years—emotionally, physically, psychologically—without any resolution, which leaves us wounded.

2. Accompanying this wounding is a *charge*, an energetic imprint, an excitation (be it positive or negative) that infiltrates our lives—especially when circumstances arise that mimic the ones in which we first were wounded.

3. This charge becomes so familiar to us—however unpleasant it may be—that it seems to be none other than just another natural part of us.

4. In our adolescent and/or adult years, *we plug this charge—our original wound-generated excitation—into sexual channels*, thereby both reliving it and finding some short-lived but strongly appealing release from it.

5. This continues, often addictively, until we awaken to what we're doing and turn toward our original wounding with compassion and fitting action.[1]

An example: Bill is strongly drawn to being overpowered sexually, with violent overtones. He assumes this is just the way he is—different strokes for different folks, right? His charge, however, isn't primarily sexual. His early years featured being heavily dominated by a raging, physically violent parent. Those were scary times for him, filled with negative excitation. But negative excitation is still excitation.

---

[1]Robert Augustus Masters, *To Be a Man* (Boulder, CO: Sounds True, 2015), 220–221.

He grew up with this unresolved sense of being dominated in his system, finding himself magnetically drawn to those through whom this early dynamic could be relived. Having eroticized this pull, he assumes he's just naturally drawn to people and situations that feature such dominance. He has sexualized being overpowered, viewing it as no more than something that certain consenting adults do. His underlying—and unattended—woundedness is left in the dark as he sexually acts out its dynamics. The release this provides briefly takes the edge off his deep-seated pain, distancing him from the abused child within.

Another example: Jill grew up in a household similar to Bill's. She also has a charge with being overpowered, but she has a much stronger charge with being safe. She entered her adulthood eroticizing her craving for safety, finding herself most sexually attracted to partners who were far from overpowering (sometimes weak and powerless) and cut off from their anger. She may eventually get bored in such "nice" relationships, but will remain hooked to the safety—however deadening it may be—provided by her partner, until she works in-depth with her conditioning.

When we bring out of our shadow the eroticized charge we still have with early-life pain, no longer directing it into sexual outlets, we're able to be compassionately present both with this charge and with the us originally subjected to such pain.

Signs of Shadow in Sexuality

Desperation. This isn't just characterized by the must in lust but also by emotional pain and frantic energy—especially in the form of anxiety. The disproportionate craving here isn't just about sexual arousal; we've attached exaggerated importance to getting sexual, and we're ignoring the distraught child in us, which just amplifies our desperation, building up enough edgy excitation in our system to seemingly necessitate sexual expression and release.

The greater our craving to distract ourselves from our suffering, the greater our craving for sexual arousal and release tends to be.

Eroticitis. This means excessive or obsessive interest in sexual activity, opportunity, or possibility. It's commonly mistaken for a strong libido. It provides distraction from the wounds that underlie and animate it. Pornography is the business end of eroticitis.

Attributing an exaggerated liberating power to sexual activity. This reaction is common, because sex can temporarily expand our boundaries, briefly take our minds off our troubles, and discharge some of our tension for a short while. But this pseudo-liberation doesn't add up to real freedom and, in fact, can bind us more tightly to sex and the release it promises. We can get addicted both to sexual release and to the energetic buildup that precedes it. This is akin to putting on a painfully tight pair of shoes and wearing them until they just have to be taken off, to our immense relief. The tighter the shoes, the greater and more energetically satisfying the release.

Acting as if being sexually showy or seductive is a sign of liberation. This kind of behavior is often taken to indicate some sort of empowerment—or perhaps even spiritual status—when what it actually demonstrates is a lack of real power. Underlying this behavior is a craving for attention, at the center of which is the neglected or abused child we once were and are now unknowingly identified with.

Normalizing "kinky" or aberrant sexual behavior. There's an overly tolerant, blind acceptance going on here, along with an unwillingness to consider and explore such behavior's originating factors, most of which are nonsexual. For example, we might dramatically play out power dynamics during sex (as in BDSM) without connecting the dots between it and unresolved power issues from our early years (with the original charge from this now being channeled into sexual contexts).

Labeling anything that's sexually unconventional as "sex-positive." This reaction basically means that we don't want to question or investigate what we're up to sexually. It's as if we're sure we have no shadow sexually; we're just a consenting adult engaging in healthy sex. Here we may confuse having clear sexual boundaries with being sexually repressed.

Projection. Men who claim to be victims of feminine sexual allure are projecting onto women the responsibility for the amplification of their sexual arousal. The dark extreme of such thinking is "If she brings out the beast in me, then why shouldn't I pounce on her?" The work here is to take charge of our charge, assuming full responsibility for what we do with our sexual arousal.

Women who have sex with men when they don't want to—and don't have to—may act as if they're powerless to do otherwise. They're projecting their power onto the man, disowning it. And they might use their powerlessness as an allure, much like their mothers may have done to pacify an otherwise aggressive or dissatisfied husband. In any case, they're simply keeping all too much of their power in their shadow.

Expecting sex to create connection. Many of us employ sex to generate a sense of connection, but this eventually backfires as we get more and more reliant on sex for this. *The key here is to connect first, then be sexual, so that sex is an expression of already-present connection.* Rather than burdening sex with the obligation to make us feel more connected to the other, we could instead bring our difficulties in feeling connected out of our shadow and work through them.

Expecting sex to make us feel better or more secure. This pressure puts an overemphasis on sex and diverts us from facing and working with the roots of our unhappiness and insecurity. What if we were to connect deeply first and then allow sex to be an expression of such connection, such communion? Deep sex doesn't promise happiness but *begins* with already-present happiness and intimate relational communion.

Needing to use fantasy during sex. If we have to fantasize in order to have "good" sex, we're then not so much interested in sex as we are in generating mind games that mostly aim to maximize erotic sensation. It's easy to normalize sexual fantasies that aren't really expressions of our sexuality but rather expressions of our unresolved wounding. When we're caught up in fantasy during sex, we maroon ourselves from intimate connection. And when we strip such fantasies of their erotic elements, the storyline that remains features the psychological and emotional underpinnings—the nonsexual factors—that first drove us into "needing to" fantasize during sex.

Being or becoming emotionally disconnected during sex. Such disconnection commonly gets obscured by whatever sexual activity is happening, including when the heated exchanges of erotic arousal get confused with emotional intimacy. When we're emotionally cut off while being sexual, we keep what's happening in the shallows, no matter how heated our sexual activity may be.

Avoiding being vulnerable during sex. Here, we're avoiding seeing and admitting what's really going on during sex besides erotic interplay. We're keeping our heart in the shadows, compensating for our loss of real connection by losing ourselves in sexual sensation (and perhaps also amplifying such sensation through staying invulnerable and using arousal fantasies). What can help here, in part, is maintaining mutual eye contact during sex while we slow down and get more present.

Overemphasizing orgasm. The greater our pain (including that of relational unhappiness) and the pressure of our unresolved wounds, the greater our investment may be in having orgasms—and the more, the better. Instead of going for orgasms, make heartfelt, emotionally vulnerable connection your priority; drop into being orgasmic, making moment-to-moment room for love-suffused sensuality and sexuality that's not goal oriented.

Hyperfocusing on certain body parts. This compartmentalizing mostly zeroes in on erogenous zones—putting a pronounced frame around them—but may also include other parts of the body. There's a comforting disconnection here from the actual person; we get to bypass any relational complications. This tendency dates back to an early need to have something to strongly fixate on in troubled times; the charge with this need was eroticized later in life.

Engaging in sex when we really don't want to. Here sex is a kind of bargaining tool, as when we get better treatment from another because we've just had sex with them. Or we may try to spice up our sex life, erotically manipulating ourselves rather than exploring the roots of what's not working in our relationship.

Using sex to discharge unwanted emotional energy. When we use sex simply to relieve ourselves, we're basically reducing our partner to an outhouse for the emotional overload we're emptying ourselves of.

■

Exploring the shadow elements associated with our sexuality is an immensely rewarding adventure. Doing so allows us to release sex from the expectations with which we've burdened it and to stop employing it to act out our unhealed wounds. Then, rather than using sex to try to create connection, we allow it to be a full-bodied, mutually transparent celebration of *already-present* happiness, trust, and connection.

12 OUR SPIRITUALITY

SPIRITUALLY SPEAKING, we can have quite a shadow, including the denial that we have a shadow.

The Eastern wisdom traditions that have become so popular in Western culture since the 1960s don't include shadow work. Nor do Western religions. Many spiritual paths equate spirituality with light, commonly attaching a negative connotation to whatever is assumed to be "negative" or "dark." The price we've paid for not examining our shadow in relation to our spirituality is enormous, leaving us divided and cut off from our full humanity, often associating being spiritual with being removed from or above everyday embodied life.

It doesn't matter how spiritually developed we are if we remain ignorant of our shadow, staying blind to our less-than-noble motivations for getting spiritual, unaware of how what's unhealthy or immature in us shows up in—and often is masked by—our spirituality. All too often spirituality is a flight from shadow, an attempt to escape what we're keeping in the dark. Such spirituality is little more than avoidance in holy robes, wherein dissociation masquerades as transcendence.

Spiritual Bypassing

At the core of spirituality's shadow is *spiritual bypassing*, meaning the use of spiritual beliefs and practices to avoid dealing with painful feelings, relational challenges, unresolved wounds, and developmental needs.

Wherever we come across spirituality, we also come across spiritual bypassing. And how could we not, given that many people are drawn to spiritual practices and paths not just due to spiritual longing but also because of psychological and emotional issues they don't want to face?

The signs of spiritual bypassing include:

Exaggerated detachment. We witness whatever is going on from too much of a distance. What's in our shadow here is our attachment to keeping ourselves removed from worldly matters, relationship concerns, uncomfortable emotions, and so on. Within this realm of pseudo-transcendence, there's no intimacy with what has supposedly been transcended. (To truly transcend something means, in part, remaining intimately associated with it, so that when we go beyond it we don't turn away from it; we're including it in the circle of our being.)

Emotional dissociation. This frequently masquerades as equanimity. Such disconnection from our emotions, especially our painful ones, may be seen as a kind of spiritual virtue, a sign of being above the fray of ordinary life. The implicit avoidance here is usually left unacknowledged, tucked far into our shadow.

Devaluing the personal. Plenty of spirituality is overly concerned with transcending the personal, which it may equate with mere egoity, as if the ego is in the way of spiritual realization. We may be advised to "drop our story" or be told "it's just our story," both of which imply that focusing on and exploring our personal history and dynamics are an impediment to our spiritual evolution. But the personal is *not* in the way and is not lesser than the transpersonal. *When transcendence of the personal takes precedence over intimacy with the personal, spiritual bypassing is inevitable.*

Pathologizing anger. Much of spirituality treats anger as a hindrance, something negative, an unwholesome state. Such anger-phobia pollutes spiritual practice, leading to a loss of power, weak boundaries, and a lack of relational authenticity and depth. Spiritual teachings that equate anger with aggression, ill will, and hatred do their followers a huge disservice. If we're on a spiritual path that doesn't equate anger with anything valuable, we're likely going to shame ourselves when we feel angry, because expressing anger supposedly indicates that we're not doing well spiritually. But anger that coexists with compassion, even when it's fierily expressed, is healthy. The cultivation of such anger can't arise in atmospheres that demonize anger.

Overemphasizing being positive. This behavior strands us from our shadow and its riches. Such sunny-side-up spirituality keeps us in the shallows, impaled on exaggerated optimism. Here, we're being negative about our negativity. Trying to be really positive, upbeat, unrelentingly optimistic disconnects us from much of what's occurring, dividing and therefore disempowering us, regardless of our efforts toward oneness.

Blind compassion. This is essentially neurotic or overdone tolerance in caring's robes. It's confrontation-phobic. When we're caught up in blind compassion and treated badly by another or by a group, we make excuses for their abuse. We ask ourselves what the situation says about us—how did we attract it, how did we create it, and so on—and leave whoever has mistreated us off anything resembling a hot seat. We may even act as if not holding them accountable is a sign of our spiritual development. In blind compassion, we easily slip into being super nice, doing whatever we can to not rock the boat.

Weak or overly porous boundaries. Having such boundaries is part of blind compassion and anger-phobia. Here, we even may equate a lack of boundaries with being "open" or spiritually advanced.

Delusions of being more awakened than we actually are. Such misguided thinking helps keep us removed from any consideration of shadow, reinforcing our denial that we're denying our own darkness. Unfounded or premature claims to spiritual attainment are common in much of contemporary spirituality. What's animating such claims—unresolved hurt, low self-esteem, childhood suppressions, and so on—remains deep in our shadow, until at least some degree of disillusionment sets in. When we've had an authentic spiritual awakening, we may make spiritual real estate out of this, acting as if we've somehow "arrived," being blinded by the light of our experience.

Making judging wrong. This is just us judging ourselves or others for judging. Who doesn't judge? Judging comes with having a mind; whenever we're evaluating something, we're judging. What matters is what we *do* with our judging mind.

Viewing the body as just a container for the real us. This perspective not only devalues our body but also unquestioningly assumes that we're actually *in* a body. My deepest sense is that who and what we truly are is not *in* a body but is being expressed *as* a body. This realization helps cut through our looking down on our body as a mere "it" or container, or an incarnational inconvenience. We may talk of being trapped in our body, but what we're really trapped by is our refusal to fully embody ourselves, to come alive right down to our toes, to honor our body as a wondrous expression of who and what we truly are.

For more, see my book *Spiritual Bypassing*.

We need a spirituality that embraces deep-diving shadow work, that's committed to being at home with *all* that we are: high and low, dark and light, free and not-so-free. In such spirituality, the personal, inter-personal, and transpersonal fruitfully coexist.

Real spirituality doesn't demonize darkness. It dynamically coexists with psychological and emotional work, making ample room for illuminating and making good use of whatever is in our shadow. Such spirituality is centered by a deeply embodied, full-blooded awakening that includes *all* that we are. In it there's no dissociation from our humanness, no flight from feeling. It's far from dry! It's not an escape but an arrival, featuring the cultivation of intimacy with everything—*everything!*—that we are.

13 OUR FEAR OF DEATH

BEING AT PEACE with the *idea* of death may give us the sense that we have no fear of death. But this fear is rooted so deeply in us that we may have no awareness of it, regardless of how much room it occupies in our shadow. Unconscious death anxiety is far more common than we might think.

Death terrifies ego-occupied us. No wonder we dress up corpses as if they were going to a social outing; no wonder we often go to absurd lengths to keep the almost-dead alive for as long as possible; no wonder so many believe in an afterlife that's an eternal, death-free holiday for "I." The fear of loss, the fear of major change, the fear of personal disaster are all rooted in the fear of death—whatever threatens our survival and not necessarily just physically.

The good news is that the fear of death, when fully brought out of our shadow and into our heart, deepens our intimacy with both death and life, and shifts our basic orientation toward death away from fear. There's no solid consensus on what death actually is—other than complete biological cessation. But considering what it *might* be for us, beyond us being terminally inconvenienced, can bring us closer to it, without making it any less unknown. "Ashes to ashes," we might declare, but what else might there be—what unsuspected blueprints or seeds? There are no definitive answers to these questions, but there's the possibility of open-ended inquiry and courageous curiosity, a deepening of our intimacy with the great Mystery of death—and living.

Avoiding death deadens us. Death is part of life, making possible more life, more evolution, more ways of being. Life is a near-death experience—literally. Is death ever really that far away? To avoid death is to avoid what it makes possible, slowly but surely numbing us to life. Meditating on our mortality is far from a morbid practice. It actually enlivens us, making our living more vivid, more relevant and real, so that what really matters to us now *really* matters.

The opposite of death isn't life but birth. The door swings both ways: we enter, live for a time, and then exit. We take our first breath and, not so long after, take our last. In between is our lifetime, basically a momentary display of color, sound, movement, feeling, awareness, and complex dramatization in which we're ever-so-briefly immersed. We might pity insects that have a maximum lifetime of just a few days, but we're in the same basic position from the perspective of what animates the infinite galaxies of form. Recognizing this at our core is immensely and wonderfully humbling; we see our extraordinary tininess and brevity in the boundless presence of all that is, and we end up not in despair or existential shadowlands but in deeply sobering awe, embodying an openness that holds it all.

Death serves our entry into such openness. Death leaves no one out. We all get the same opportunity. How prepared we are for this is a central element in how we differ. Life outlives us, yet we are life. This turns from a paradox into unspeakable truth when we cease turning away from death, no longer pushing its bare reality into our shadow.

The Shadow of Death

"Yea, though I walk through the valley of the shadow of death, I will fear no evil." This passage, taken from one of the best-known Psalms, alludes to the felt presence and reality of death, its darkness dramatized through the vast spread of its shadow.

When it comes to shadows that can be cast, none eclipse that of death. There's much, though, about death and dying that doesn't just cast a shadow but also occupies *our* shadow.

Foremost here is the *denial* of death, in which the naked reality of death is marginalized or pushed out of sight. Death then is treated the way the Victorian era treated sex—as something behind closed doors, something to cover up as much as possible, something that happens to *others*. The denial of death takes many forms:

The compulsive need to look young. This compulsion overvalues youthful looks, regarding them as hugely preferable to an aged appearance. Consider wrinkles: the skinny on skin is the tighter and more unblemished, the better. Ads for antiwrinkle creams and Botoxed, smooth-skinned spreads overpopulate many a popular magazine. Looking young—and thus seemingly far from death and dying—gets an almost universal nod over looking old, including in funeral-home corpses. What's in the shadows here is openly faced, maskless aging, along with a compassionate view of our visual weathering.

The compulsive need to stay young. This compulsion overvalues acting youthful, giving much more credence to youthful-seeming achievements than to the achievements of real elderhood, such as wisdom and equanimity. Also included here are things that help provide a relatively convincing sense of being younger than we are, such as having a much younger wife—anything to provide the sense that we haven't aged all that much. What's in the shadows here is the embracing of the shift in capacities that comes with aging, and the acceptance and celebration of the further reaches of aging.

Leaving unchallenged the decreasing visibility of older women. There's a cultural marginalizing of postmenopausal and elderly women. Their aging is generally taken to mean that their beauty is declining. (Those who are still considered beautiful usually have taken strong measures, including plastic surgery, to look young.) There still are far fewer film roles for women past the age of sixty than for men of the same age, as if the sight of an elderly woman carries less weight, less attractive force, than the sight of a man of similar age. What's in the shadows here is the fear of death in the form of women who openly show the signs of aging.

The funeral industry. The denial here isn't of outright death per se, but of the undressed reality of death. Death has been removed from the home, much like birth was removed from the home until the last three or four decades in contemporary Western culture. Corpses are embalmed to make them to look more lifelike and often dressed as if they're going to a party or business meeting. There's a prevailing sense of protecting the deceased from the elements and decomposition, as if we're projecting onto the dead the notion that they're still alive, still not *really* dead. The good news is that there's an increasing swing from funeral homes to home funerals, paralleling the move to more home births. What's in the shadows here is the fear of death, especially as a visible phenomenon.

Striving for immortality. At the core of this striving is the avoidance of fully facing our mortality. The irony is that when we cease avoiding our mortality and become intimate with it, we're brought into contact with the deathless. This doesn't mean that we live forever, but we understand that what exists forever isn't truly apart from us. Implicit in this understanding isn't personal immortality but the never-ending reality of bare is-ness. What's in the shadows here is the fear of our mortality.

Acting as if death is a failure. This form of denial is illustrated by efforts, medical and otherwise, to keep the dying alive no matter what the cost. In this perspective there often is a notion that death is a disease, an error in the human system, something that will someday be overcome. In settings featuring this view, there's little room to die with dignity. What's in the shadows here is the naturalness and, even more so, the inevitability of death.

Treating death as a morbid subject. Keeping death out of polite conversation by changing the subject allows us to avoid it. It's time to bring death out of the closet—and not just in therapy sessions or at the time of a loved one's dying and death. What's in the shadows here is our fear of death—with its presenting surface being our fear of endings.

Using euphemisms for death. When we speak of the dead as having "passed away," "gone to a better place," "transitioned," and so on, we're usually one step removed from the bare fact that they've died.

What's in the shadows here is our investment in thinking that death is somehow less than death, that it's a kind of transit lounge en route to a new destination. Not that we can say with certainty that nothing happens to us after we die—but to simply believe in this as a way of reducing the impact of actual death is quite different than directly experiencing some sort of postdeath continuity.

Unquestioned belief in an afterlife. Though there's no definitive cross-cultural answer to the question of what happens to us after we die, regardless of the certainties of religion and atheism, many still rigidly adhere to a belief in an afterlife. If we leave this belief unexamined, we leave ourselves less open to death and what might follow it. What's in the shadows here is our attachment to not ending. The Mystery of death transcends all ideas of death.

Unquestioned disbelief in an afterlife. This is the opposite of the previous belief—a concretized belief that death is nothing more than annihilation. This seemingly tough, no-nonsense stance may seem brave in the face of our mortality, but it's not so brave in its avoidance of the possible transpersonal or spiritual dimensions of death. What occupies the shadow here is the fear of openly facing death and its inherent Mystery, as well as the edgeless Mystery of our real identity.

Narcissism. Narcissism is epidemic in cultures that overemphasize individuality. In narcissism, we keep ourselves fortified against anything that might render us vulnerable, such as letting ourselves openly feel the reality of our mortality and the ever-present proximity of death. What's in the shadows here is empathy, vulnerability, and a sense of community.

Emotional numbness. We can blunt the felt reality of our mortality by cutting ourselves off from emotional depth. If we're numb enough, dissociated enough, we may think that we have no fear of death, no death anxiety. But we've really just driven our fear of death further into the dark. What's in the shadows here is our fear of death and a fully alive emotional life, along with our attachment to excessive detachment and the immunity it promises.

Aversion to grief. Ours is a culture drowning in unexpressed grief. When faced with grief, so many assume they're being strong—including being strong for others—when they suppress their grief, allowing themselves only a brief leakage of tears. When we grieve fully, our hearts break open and the feeling of deep loss runs through us with wild abandon. We may get angry; we may wail; we may cry our guts out; we may feel crazy then peaceful, then hugely spacious, and on and on. Grief isn't a tidy emotion, and if we associate being in control with looking good, we aren't going to feel much like opening to our grief. Our culture is averse to real mourning, to emotionally expressing—*really* expressing—what a particular death means to us. What's in the shadows here is our naked heart and vulnerability, along with the shame that might accompany full-out emotional rawness.

Stopping short of living fully and deeply. Such a life may sound good on paper, but given that it inevitably brings us into more intimate contact with death and mortality, we may only partially give ourselves to it. What's in the shadows here is our fear of the consequences of being our full self.

To Bring the Fear of Death Out of the Shadow

Identify and explore your assumptions about death. Stand a short distance from your assumptions about death; bring a fresh eye to them and their origins. Write them down. This may bring forth more uncertainty regarding the nature of death, but it will help open you more fully to the Mystery of death—and life.

Compassionately hold your desire to avoid death. Bring this desire into your heart, as if cradling a distressed child whom you love. You're not trying to get rid of this desire but rather to draw it out of your shadow.

Be with your mortality daily. Don't just think about your death but feel into it, register the reality of it. Do this for a few minutes when you awaken in the morning and when you're readying yourself for sleep at night. Also do it when you're starting to fuss about the small stuff. If being with your mortality brings on anxiety, stop and hold such fearfulness as you would a frightened child you care about deeply.

Don't postpone what needs doing. Become more aware of where you are putting your life on hold and challenge the apparent necessity of doing this, including bringing to it the perspective of your own mortality. Consider what you would want to do, what you would want to complete, if you found out that you had only a year left to live.

Fully explore your shadow. Develop intimacy with its elements; bring them all out of the dark, including the reality of death, the fear of death, the inevitability of your own demise. Everything that occupies your shadow is worth exploring and illuminating; leaving any of it out of your investigation keeps you short of being truly here. Make being aware of and working with your shadow a central practice.

Don't turn away from death. Turn toward it, with undivided attention and care. Cease treating it as a problem or as bad news only. Explore your craving for more time, realizing that more time near the end of life can be a mixed blessing—it means not only more time to live but also more time to decline.

Come deeply alive, regardless of your circumstances and age. When we fully feel life, participating in it wholeheartedly, we open not just to the wonder, beauty, pain, and glory of life but also to the vivid brevity of its forms, which include us. The more we unguardedly feel into and feel for this brevity, the more precious life becomes to us, and the more readily death serves as a potent reminder of this. Cultivating intimacy with death, with mortality, with deep loss, keeps us traveling lighter, turning impermanence into raw beauty and unspeakable revelation.

Make not-knowing more central in your life. What I mean by "not-knowing" isn't ignorance or mental fogginess but being internally open and spacious, uncluttered by any preset knowledge and comfortable with not having all the answers. Not-knowing is a state in which we're not bound by the known. The more we abide in not-knowing, the more intimate our contact with death becomes, simply because we're wide open to it, even in the most seemingly mundane of conditions, such as the movement of breath through our body.

Imagine yourself on your deathbed. Imagine you're taking your final ten or so breaths. Sense yourself letting go of your body, letting it settle into deep rest, even as you settle into boundless spaciousness, opening more and more to the core mystery of what's happening. After sufficient time with this vision—a few minutes at the very least—say a prayer that affirms what kind of death you want. For example: *May I die a peaceful and liberating death, and may I approach it with a clear mind and open heart.* Say this prayer gently. Repeat it.

Meditate daily, in ways that keep you present and grounded. Begin with a practice that helps you concentrate your focus (such as counting your breaths on the exhale, one to five, always returning to one when you forget which number you're on). Then, once your focus is relatively stable, let go of your concentrative practice and let your attention expand into formless openness, giving your undivided attention to the unknowable nature of all that is, including death. Sense yourself both as what dies and as what doesn't die—and keep this sensing nonconceptual.

Periodically view everything as already gone. For a few minutes each day, see what has seemingly solid existence as *already* undone, unraveled, gone to dust. Yes, things seen this way are still very much here, but looking at them as though they have already disintegrated brings their innate impermanence into clearer focus. The reality of the passing of all things is at the very heart of life *and is crucial to feel fully*. Attuning to this reality isn't morbid or depressing; it's simply a matter of opening as much as possible to the temporary nature of all that is.

Sense how every letting go is a kind of dying. Feel into this realization, the grief and renewal of it, the many small deaths that make up a lifetime. So much letting go passes by unseen. Consider the letting go of each exhale; we usually do this quite automatically, taking for granted that an inhale will follow. We are, in a sense, always dying into more life, dying to live.

■

What happens after death is here now, moment by moment. Intimacy with death makes this obvious; it leaves us nowhere to go other than deeper into here, no one to be other than what we essentially already are, be we in shadow or light.

This we know, not as gathered knowledge but as what's revealed when we shift from trying to figure out the Mystery of existence to recognizing ourselves as unique and uniquely evolving expressions of it. Here, staying alive as long as possible becomes secondary to dying well.

14 OUR RESISTANCE

RESISTANCE IS THE EXPRESSION—verbal or nonverbal—of our no to someone or something. It's a boundary assertion meant to protect us.

Healthy resistance protects, with adequate force, what needs protecting; unhealthy resistance *overprotects* what needs protection or protects what doesn't need any protection. In either case, resistance impedes, obstructs, defies, battles, blocks, counteracts, dissents—whatever helps strengthen the no at its core.

Our resistance often arises as a defense, however unconscious, of the child within us; it's a self-protective force we couldn't summon when we were children. It provides a functional barrier against pressures, expectations, and imprinting that weren't in our best interests as a child and that current circumstances are mimicking. As obsolete as this defense may seem to be now, it's arising because unresolved childhood wounding is surfacing within us, wounding that lacks the safety of adequate protection.

Our resistance doesn't always arise from early-life wounding. Consider a well-meaning mother who insisted that her daughter swallow vitamin pills every day and eat healthy food. Now, as an adult, her daughter often "forgets" to take her supplement capsules and finds a guilty pleasure in wolfing down junk food. This behavior may look like her choice, but her childhood resistance is in charge.

Our resistance can be straightforward, direct, obvious, and it can also be something we conceal in our shadow to keep it from being expressed.

When Resistance Is in Our Shadow

If our full no was disrespected, met with aggression, or otherwise handled badly in our early years, then it's likely that later on in life we'll have trouble saying no and standing behind it with much conviction. We'll resist saying no to things we would like to say no to, or need to say no to, but that resistance won't be straightforward. Instead, it'll show up in indirect ways, such as in passive aggression and other manipulative behavior.

Jack had a controlling, almost dictatorial father. He married Lola, who was easygoing and kind. When she nicely asks him, a skillful handyman, to take care of a repair in the house or to pick up an item from the store on his way home, Jack "forgets." She patiently tolerates this behavior for a while, but eventually she can take it no more and shows her frustration and accuses him of forgetting on purpose. He denies this, saying that he just has a bad memory and that he doesn't mean to hurt her. What's in his shadow is his resistance to doing anything that makes him feel—however remotely—like a boy under his father's command.

The more out of touch we are with our resistance, the more space it takes up in our shadow—along with our attachment to denying the existence of our resistance. Some of this attachment goes back to our early years when our expressions of resistance were met with aggression, shaming, or a loss of love.

When resistance is not out front, not directly displaying any oppositional energy, it's mostly stationed in our shadow. We might feel resistance from another but be met with their denial that they're resisting and maybe also by their assertion that we're just imagining or projecting things. The situation then stalemates, reduced to no more than their word against ours.

When we deny, deflect, or downplay the reality of our resistance to doing something, we drive much, if not all, of our anger into our shadow. Being able to back up our resistance requires strong boundaries, and these can't be maintained without having our anger on tap. When our resistance is disowned and kept out of sight, our anger is dampened, muzzled, kept on a tight leash, and its fires are present only as a distant smoldering in the darkness. Not having our anger available disempowers us, leaving us with leaky, tattered, or nonexistent boundaries.

When we won't put forth and embody a clear no, our ability to say a real yes gets seriously compromised.

Those who too easily go along with the dictates of a group—be it one's family, social circle, political party, or spiritual community—are those whose ability to tap into and fully express their no has been largely pushed into their shadow, to the point where they often have little or no idea that this is happening.

Ceasing to View Resistance as Something Wrong

Resistance is inevitable, but it isn't necessarily a problem, regardless of the negative press it often gets—especially in circles, be they mundane or spiritual, that emphasize unquestioning loyalty to an overseeing hierarchy. Saddling resistance or "being in resistance" with negative connotations simply shames those who are thus "infected." Making resistance wrong only drives it further into the shadows.

Consider someone who's part of a group that has a strongly held set of beliefs about the proper way to live. If this person questions these beliefs, they then may be viewed by others in the group, especially those in charge, as resisting the teachings and needing only to "surrender" to them. Perhaps this person is presented with various dire consequences of holding on to such "resistance." It's no surprise that they'll tend, at least for a while, to go through the motions of surrendering, perhaps garnering group and leader approval for thus demonstrating that they have let go of their resistance.

Spiritual and personal-growth teachers who tell their students that they're resisting are doing little more than resisting such resistance, keeping it at enough of a distance so as to be all but blind to its relevance and roots.

Our resistance, however rigid or socially incorrect, often may arise in our best interests, giving us a needed braking, a time-out to reconsider our options (as when we, for example, are being pressured into committing to a relationship or a group) or to simply find the resolve to remove ourselves from abusive or otherwise life-negating circumstances.

Approaching Our Resistance

The no that our resistance transmits might not be a particularly intelligent or well-informed no, but it nonetheless is clearly a no and needs to be heard as such before we get busy critiquing or marginalizing the stand it's taking. It needs to be seen and approached as more than a mere obstacle or hindrance.

There's considerable energy in resistance. Such energy may be trapped, overcontained, overcommitted to defense. But under the right conditions it can be freed and redirected so that it serves rather than hinders us.

Everyone I've worked with has shown up with two fundamental desires: the obvious one being to fully heal and be truly free, and the less obvious one being to resist this—mostly because of what it asks, and *has to ask*, of us. We'd love to have the benefits of a profoundly transformative shift in our entire being without having to go through any of the steps—especially the painful or strongly challenging ones—required for that shift. Such a wish is natural to us, at least until we understand that we're going to have to turn toward all that stuff we've resisted facing most of our life. This is when our honeymoon with make-us-feel-better spirituality and three-easy-steps psychology ends.

Resistance shouldn't be automatically dismantled, leveled, or otherwise cut down, because it may be guarding something that really needs guarding—*safeguarding*—or that at one time did. Blasting through our resistance (by means of aggressive therapeutic intervention, for example) may for a short while generate some good feelings (in much the same way that intense sexual discharge might), but in the long run it only reinforces our need to reestablish and stand behind our original resistance. Whatever it was protecting—an extremely vulnerable layer of us, for example—will call to us from deep inside to wall it in once again.

It's vital to listen closely to what our resistance is saying beyond its self-presentation. We need to feel into and illuminate the pain that underlies and animates our resistance; we need to open our heart to the wounded child within us that's at the heart of most of our resistance. We need to take better care of our resistance, neither repressing it nor acting it out. This begins with acknowledging it and bringing both it and what it's trying to protect out of our shadow so that we have a clear view of its history and constituent elements.

The Many Faces of Resistance

Procrastination. This is the practice of avoiding and needlessly delaying making a decision or taking action. It's a no-one's land of impotent promises, featuring a self-disempowerment rooted in bypassing the *now*. When we procrastinate, we remain internally divided—should I or shouldn't I?—and our attachment to putting things off is hidden in our shadow. What's especially helpful here is to face the *origins* of our fear of what might happen if we make certain decisions or take certain actions. What's often at the heart of procrastination is our inner child/teen rebelling against being controlled or told what to do.

Distraction. This is the practice of being elsewhere, of bypassing both the *now* and the *here*. Distraction is a getaway that leaves what we truly need to do in the background or out of sight. The work here is to stop distracting ourselves from our distractions and instead illuminate them and their pull on us as much as possible. Getting to intimately know our distractions, and what we're distracting ourselves from, makes it much more difficult to rationalize or cave in to them.

Addiction. This is compulsive overattachment to certain practices, substances, or beliefs. It's desire gone awry. In addiction we're resisting our true needs, keeping them in our shadow while we act out. Central to working with addiction is to compassionately encounter the addict within, developing as much intimacy with that one's underlying wounding as possible. (For more on addiction, see chapter 10.)

Defensiveness. This is the practice of aggressively blocking relational connection, usually in the name of being right. There's an exaggerated hardening or thickening of boundaries, an in-your-face resistance that may be conveyed with a smile, snarl, or absence of facial expression. Defensiveness closes the heart. It's an intimacy killer, until we play whistle-blower to our own defensiveness. To work with it is to name it, explore its underbelly, see through it, disarm it.

Self-sabotage. This is the practice of obstructing ourselves, of ensuring that we won't succeed in a particular venture. Getting in our own way without taking any responsibility for doing so is the essence of self-sabotage. There's much in our shadow here, including the neglect of our inner child, the lack of restraint we grant our rationalizing capacity, and our fear of the consequences of succeeding. When approaching our capacity for sabotaging ourselves, it's important to do so without any shaming. (For more on self-sabotage, see chapter 24.)

Guilt. This emotion features the shadow-held decision to stay emotionally divided and small. *Where shame exposes us, guilt splits us.* Part of us, fixatedly childish, does the "bad" deed, and another part, fixatedly parental, punishes us, beating us up through the voice of our inner critic. The stalemate between the two is the essence of guilt. When we're busy playing out the dramatics of guilt, we're keeping ourselves from facing what really needs to be addressed, including the pain we may have caused another. Guilt means we don't have to grow up.

Turning our pain into suffering. Pain comes with life—often inevitably so. On the other hand, suffering—by which I mean the overdramatizing of pain (as when we get overly absorbed in the story of how someone wronged us)—is optional. When we're caught up in suffering, we're not available for healing and breakthrough; yes, we're hurting, but we're also resisting that hurt. Suffering keeps all too much of our pain in our shadow. To end our suffering, we need to enter our pain. (For more on how to work with pain, see part 3.)

Deflection. Energetically speaking, this lightweight cousin of defensiveness isn't so much a wall as a flick, a redirecting of what's coming our way back onto the other. Through doing so, we get to remain intact, while the other becomes the focus, the one with the problem, the one taking the heat. When we're busy deflecting, we tend to act as if we're not doing so; we're simply trying to get through to the other. What's in the shadows here? Aggression.

Dissociation. Unhealthy separation or disconnection—spacing out, losing touch, feeling stranded from what's going on, being disembodied—often means being emotionally vacant or flat. One of the first steps in working with dissociation is to get more embodied, grounded, present.

Claims of trying. When we say that we're trying to do something, we're really saying that we're only *partially* into doing it. And being divided about it, it's therefore very likely we won't do it, at least to any significant degree. In saying that we're trying, we're cutting ourselves slack for when we don't follow through. In trying, we can make a show of proceeding, perhaps with the same sincerity we bring to New Year's resolutions, but at best we're only bringing a half-hearted approach to it.

How to Work with Your Resistance

Here are some ways you can begin working skillfully with your resistance:

Clarify its signs. Get familiar with the many ways your resistance shows up.

Name your resistance when it arises. This practice will often coincide with your times of reactivity, so learn to recognize the connections that exist between your resistance and reactivity. Name your resistance as soon as you become aware of it (perhaps saying "resistance," "my resistance is here," or "I'm feeling resistant"). If possible, also name what your resistance is attempting to safeguard (such as your right to be respected).

Don't shame yourself for your resistance. Remember how natural it is to have resistance and how the potential problem isn't your resistance itself but how you handle it.

Identify it without attaching any negative evaluation to it. Treat your resistance as something not to be condemned or discarded but as something to be curious about, something worth exploring.

Identify what purpose it has served—and is serving. What has it been protecting, or attempting to protect, in you?

Explore its origins. When and how did this resistance first appear in you? What was it in response to? Connect the dots between past and present—and not just intellectually. Exploring what your resistance is protecting, and the origins and history of that, can be facilitated by a suitably skilled psychotherapist.

Personify what it's guarding. Do this practice at least some of the time. For example, if you identify fearfulness as something that's behind your resistance, somewhere in the shadows, you can imagine this emotional state as a fearful child and relate to him or her as if you're a lovingly protective parent.

Give it emotional and somatic expression. At the right time, give your resistance a voice through fitting sound and movement (such as thrusting your hands out as if pushing something unwanted away). Keep this simple: don't look for any thought-out articulation; go for a fully alive *no*. The point is for you to express your resistance with as little inhibition as possible, making sure that you do so in a setting that feels sufficiently safe and/or private.

Bring as much compassion as you can to your resistance. Do this, however, without leaving your resistance unchallenged or overtolerated.

Treat your resistance not as an "it" but as a part of you, just as deserving of care as any other aspect of you.

15 OUR HONESTY

WHEN *WHAT* **WE'RE SAYING** and *how* we're saying it aren't congruent—not in natural alignment—our shadow isn't just in the neighborhood but in our face. And though those around us likely register this communicative discord, they may overlook or tolerate it when they have a strong enough desire to unquestioningly believe what we're expressing (so as to not rock the boat, ruffle any feathers, or issue any kind of challenge).

For example, if someone is professing love for us in a situation that really calls for it, without actually showing any love for us, we may take their words as veracity because we ache to hear such words from them, all the while pressing the mute button on our bullshit detector. Even if we do attune to our doubt about what the other is insisting is true, we might then put ourselves down for having such doubt, attributing it to some failing in us. We might scold ourselves for not trusting their words, and thereby give our inner critic the go-ahead to lay into us. What we're pushing into our shadow here is our intuition.

"You're my woman, honey. Love you!" Nick tells Julie each morning as he leaves for work. She feels uneasy after he leaves, but also judges herself for doubting him: "I'm so damn insecure! I need to trust my man and stop being so silly." She grew up in a home where she could feel the tension between her parents, but when she voiced her concern, they insisted that everything was fine. She learned to not trust her intuition, the guidance of which mostly got lodged in her shadow. Not so long after she spoke self-deprecatingly to her best friend about how much she hated it when she got insecure, Nick emptied their bank account and moved to Mexico with his secretary.

When another's words don't match their emotional state and degree of relational resonance with us, something else is being conveyed that remains largely in the dark—something that speaks of matters other than what's being shared. To openly communicate our sense that this is happening, especially in our closest relationships, is a big, courageous step.

To recognize the lack of authenticity in our own speech and still deny it, even when our intimate other or a close friend is compassionately pointing it out to us, is a dangerous practice. It erodes the trust in our relationship, leaving us isolated and self-righteous, turning not toward our shadow but away from it.

Honesty is essential, but there's more to honesty than meets the eye. What's out front—the factual, straightforward presentation—may have a hidden side, residing in our shadow. If we're being honest about what we want in a particular situation, are we also being honest about what's driving such want or what we're perhaps hoping that our honesty might bring our way? That is, are we being honest about what may be in our shadow in this sort of circumstance? Are we even considering the possibility of a deeper layer of honesty?

An example: We really want to help another in need and make ourselves available for them, putting our heart and full energy into it. We're sincere, and a bond quickly deepens between us and the other. What we don't see is the connection between this helpful action and our thwarted longing as a child to help a sibling who was being abused. We were powerless to help then, but we can help now. This shadow element generates an *exaggerated* emphasis on helping the other, leading to a codependency that will be very hard to untangle until we wake up to the deeper layers animating our desire to help.

We need to take a deeper look at our yes—or consent—in any given situation to see to what degree, if any, it's arising from our wounding, our go-to behavioral patterns, our desire to reap the benefits of getting something *we* want from another by saying yes to what they want. Real honesty isn't just about being transparent, for we can use our capacity for transparency for far-from-healthy ends, such as when we enlist openness and vulnerability in the service of seducing another. We can unnecessarily hurt another with our supposed honesty and take no responsibility for its impact, barricading ourselves behind such assertions as "I'm just telling you how I see you" or "You said to share my truth. So what's your problem?"

When we make too much of a virtue out of honesty, we're likely overlooking our less-than-flattering motives for our "radical" honesty, such as:

Overpowering the other. Here we use the impact of our delivery—the content and expression of our honesty—to obstruct or otherwise diminish the power of the other. We might, for example, say that we don't like the meal that the other person has prepared, and we say this with enough of an edge to hurt them. If this upsets them, we might respond, "I'm just telling you how I feel. If it bothers you, that's your issue." When we're in this mode, our "honesty" lacks empathy and is far from brave.

Needing to stay in control. With this strategy, we use honesty in ways that disempower the other person specifically to allow us to remain in control. Truly exposing our wanting to be in control would be a vulnerable undertaking, which could leave us out of control.

Fortifying our self-esteem. Here, we give ourselves status points for being able to speak so honestly. We may have felt deflated because we were shamed when we were younger, and now we find a compensatory, gratifying sense of self-inflation—a not-so-healthy pride—through our shows of honesty.

Embellishing our psychological and spiritual resumés. Unchecked egocentricity can masquerade as the honest one, the straight shooter, especially when doing so carries a certain psychological or spiritual authority.

Needing to impress the other. It's not uncommon to use an outfront self-presentation as a means of reinforcing our sense of being somebody special, somebody impressive. We may find a certain status, for example, in being blunt, finding that others hold us in significant esteem for it.

Getting what we want. Honesty can be used as relational leverage. It can be manipulation in truth-telling's robes. When we use it this way, we're far from honest, insofar as we're not revealing what we're really up to (such as staying in control). The other may feel manipulated, but when they voice this feeling, we likely meet them with statements such as "You just can't handle the truth" or "You're avoiding looking at yourself."

■

True honesty—significantly awakened and unguarded self-disclosure—is centered by our ongoing commitment to recognizing, naming, and not acting out those motivations that we've kept in our shadow. Let's be honest about our honesty; rather than just taking it as an unquestioned good, let's transparently expose whatever motivations may be underlying our expression of honesty. Doing so increases our capacity for healthy connection with others, making their relationship with us a safer place for their self-expression.

16 CHOICE

CHOICE ISN'T NECESSARILY what it appears to be. We may think we're making a choice, but all too often it's our conditioning—in the form of our unexamined shadow material—that's making the choice.

To what extent are our choices making us? Are they anything more than conditioned preferences being automatically given a green light? How can we legitimately be said to have freedom of choice if we're not aware of and in charge to at least some degree of our choice-making capacity? This isn't so much a philosophical consideration as an existential one, asking that we not strand ourselves in the debate about free will versus determinism but instead enter the depths of which such debate is but the presenting surface.

It's very humbling to recognize the extent to which our conditioning—especially our shadow-bound conditioning—has been making our picks while we've been busy unquestioningly assuming that we're free to choose. One domain in which this is dramatically evident is choosing a partner. We often pick someone who fits those aspects of our conditioning that we have the most charge with, be that charge—that compelling excitation—positive, negative, or a mix of both. We don't consider where our choice of a partner is emerging from in us. Instead, we let ourselves be carried along by our charge with the situation, which may itself be amplified by sexual energy and expectation.

A common example is that of someone who had an emotionally distant parent and as a child longed for that parent's love, attention, and full availability. The sheer intensity, the underlying aching, of this unrequited longing made and makes for a strong charge in their system, however negative or distressing that childhood excitation might have originally been. This person reaches adulthood without having recognized and faced this shadow-bound emotional charge and finds themselves drawn to those who are, posthoneymoon, clearly not available emotionally and who resist doing anything about it.

The excitement that initially characterizes such a relationship is generally just the eroticizing of the original charge, which stems from being neglected, feeling unwanted, and yearning for a love that seemed so close and yet was so far away. The neglected child in the shadows is actually automatically picking, or magnetically zeroing in on, the partner-to-be based on their lack of availability and their *potential* to become truly available.

So unresolved childhood pain, in conjunction with the charge that goes with it, does the choosing, and will continue to do so partner after partner until one awakens to this dynamic. Once we begin observing rather than acting out the pull in this area, we become less and less seducible by the conditioning behind it.

Exploring Our Choice-Making Capacity

Choice isn't just a matter of having some options before us and picking one. We need to become aware of our actual choice-making capacity. Otherwise our conditioning—and in particular, that which remains unilluminated—does the choosing, all the while masquerading as us. Our shadow here is comprised of (1) the conditioning that's generating the choices (not consciously but mechanically), and (2) our *identification* with that very conditioning—our unquestioning alignment with it and the preferences that come along with it. When we lose ourselves in our conditioning, letting it possess us, our freedom of choice is truly an illusion. At such times, our shadow elements are generating our choices, regardless of how adult we appear.

Research has shown that having many choices about something can be paralyzing. Two kinds of applesauce don't make for a problem, but a dozen kinds can. The appraisal of the dozen options doesn't sharpen our scanning and considering capacities but rather dulls them. We can only consider or evaluate so much input at any one time; too much simply overwhelms us. This pressure is made worse if we have a history of associating choice with danger or loss, such as when we didn't choose the "right" way to be around a difficult or abusive parent and we got punished as a result.

So do we have any choice around the actual process of making choices? Yes, but only if we know our conditioning well, having brought it out of our shadow *and* begun to actively work with it emotionally and somatically.

If our habit is to turn away from our pain, seeking distraction from it, then *in* our turning toward that very pain we're making a crucial choice—a choice that comes not from our conditioning but from our core of being, our essential individuality. When we've done this for a while, so that it feels more natural to turn toward what we used to turn away from, a paradox arises: The more we awaken, and the more we know ourselves and our shadow, the more it seems that we have no choice but to continue turning toward it. And this option doesn't feel like entrapment but rather liberation. *Then the core necessity implicit in a given situation dictates the choice—or optimal move—and we simply cooperate with that.*

Consider newborns. They don't choose to do what they do; they simply do it in an automatic or reflexive response to whatever is arising. They clearly have an awareness, but it's not characterized by choice-making. A felt sense of necessity directs things. This is also true of us at our most mature, but now it's a *conscious* process. At such times we're fine with letting necessity call the shots; we then no more choose to move a certain way than does a pond choose to ripple a certain way when a pebble breaks its surface.

Choices Without a Chooser

Freedom may seem to be a matter of having choices, but it's actually more about seeing through our preference-making mechanisms. It's not that our preferences go away as we mature—or even should go away—but that we're no longer enslaved to them. It's also helpful to remember that *we don't choose our preferences.*

Our conditioning, if left unexamined, makes the picks. If we identify with our conditioning then we'll think that *we* are making the picks, and that in doing so we're exercising our free will. This belief only keeps us on automatic pilot. However, if our response to our conditioning is sufficiently conscious, we have an opportunity to break free of the "rules" of our in-house entrapment. Our circumstances may remain the same, but we're now relating to them very differently. We're in the trap but not trapped, so to speak.

An uncluttered, compassionately embodied wakefulness is probably the ideal environment for the recognition of "best move" responses, because in such a state we see our shadow and we're not run by it. But is there not a choice involved in accessing such wakefulness? Yes, but it's *a choice without a chooser*, a choice without a self-conscious indwelling entity making it all happen. That is, there's no sense of an internal somebody who, having weighed the pros and cons of being so wakefully aware, has now picked the option of being thus aware.

The deepest knowing doesn't choose, and yet out of it optimal choices are made—choices that aren't really choices in any conventional sense but rather lucid obedience to the fundamental necessities of any given situation. This may sound passive, but it's actually dynamically active, asking for a moment-to-moment attunement that keeps us alert, focused, spacious, and fully present.

There's no dissociation from responsibility here, no playing victim to the flow or necessity of things. Choices occur—*our* choices, regardless of how they arise—and we hold ourselves accountable for them, not blaming fate, our parents, or our conditioning, and we pay consistently close attention to whatever impact such choices may have.

Our choices, in many cases, may not be made by us, but without us they can't be made. We can stand apart from them, we can recognize their origins and the degree to which our conditioning has shaped them, but we can't deny ownership of them or responsibility for them. They await our lucid participation, making us as we make them.

Choose to choose well.

17 EVIL

ANY EXPLORATION OF SHADOW, if gone into far enough, will likely come up against the notion of evil.

Historically related to as a taken-for-granted reality—part of the human condition—evil nowadays has become a questionable notion for some, stored in the shadier outbacks of moral relativism. Yes, the context of any activity that might be considered evil is very important to take into account, but if we overfocus on such considerations, we run the risk of insufficiently addressing activities that by most accounts deserve to be labeled as evil. Evil doesn't have to be an overliteralized reality brandished by religious or ethnocentric fundamentalists, all but devoid of context. Nor does it have to be a term best avoided, such as God or anything else smacking of absolutism, pinned down by disembodied contextual concerns like a desiccated museum specimen.

Evil is dehumanizing belief, intent, or activity in the ugly extreme, featuring an utter absence of empathy and at least some degree of satisfaction in its perpetration.

Evil isn't necessarily synonymous with a lack of intelligence and rationality. It can wear many faces. But whatever its appearance, it remains something that we can ill afford to ignore. The more we try to push it aside, cover it up, or pretend that it's not really there, the more it surfaces.

Viewing evil as a merely relative term (one person's terrorist is another person's freedom fighter) gives us some remove from it, so that we don't have to mention it by name or get stuck trying to traverse the slippery stepping-stones of moral dilemmas that feature behaviors we abhor. We shuffle evil to a conceptual bin that has no real place for it—other than perhaps in the not-so-sure file—which keeps us "safely" removed or dissociated from the bare reality and horror of the sort of things commonly labeled "evil."

The ingredients for evil—the capacities to dehumanize, get violent, rationalize anything, be cut off from any empathy—exist in all of us. So too does the emotion of schadenfreude, in which we take pleasure in others' suffering. This emotion isn't evil in itself; we may squirm in admitting its presence in us, but it's not harmful when kept in check. But just as anger can be mishandled enough so as to become violence, schadenfreude can be mishandled enough so as to become, in conjunction with extreme aggression and disgust, the emotional bedrock of evil.

It's crucial not to turn away from the reality of collective evil. We need to deepen our awareness of how it can insinuate its way into those who are unaware of it or who view it as something other than evil. Think of how Nazism invaded and colonized German culture, masquerading as something ennobling and restorative to the German psyche. Think of how slavery was able thrive in the United States, justified as economically necessary and supported by the "scientific" view that black people were uniquely suited to be slaves. Think of corporate greed, so widespread as to seem normal to many, eating its way into us even as we numb ourselves to it. Letting in collective evil is often just a matter of taking in its propaganda, in much the same way as we absorb cultural information on a daily basis. Evil may not be digestible, but it can be made edible; throw enough masking additives into bad food, and we may unquestioningly swallow it.

Evil isn't going away just because we discount its reality or only gaze upon it for scattered moments. However buried in our shadow the ingredients for evil may be, they're still there, able to mix and sprout much more easily than we may think. Start with some contempt, amplify it with dehumanizing intent, and throw in a convincing rationale for proceeding further, and seedlings of evil will start crowding out the finer stuff in your garden.

Evil at essence is violently acted-out, extreme separation trauma, a severe splitting off from our humanity, gone over the edge of sanity, channeled into activities that satisfyingly dramatize and legitimize our pathological apartness from whom or what we would do injury to (as in the extremes of nationalistic fervor). Though evil may not appear crazy or demented—it can be hyperrational, emotionally unperturbed in circumstances that would horrify the great majority of us—it is insanity in dark bloom.

If we don't face our own capacity for evil, whatever its scale, we simply reinforce its presence in ourselves and in others. We leave it unchallenged except perhaps in others whose extreme behavior is safe to label as evil, or at least as perverse or very, very wrong.

Evil is us operating as if our heart has been cut out and replaced with a block of black ice. Evil is us standing so far apart from others that we see them as less than human and no more deserving of care than the cockroach we've just crushed under our heel. Evil is the eviscerated soul running amok, a machete in one hand and a declaration of condemnation in the other.

How to Relate to Evil

Begin by acknowledging evil, regardless of how it may be contextualized. Feel into it—feel its core of cemented contempt, rationalized sadism, and extreme estrangement from care. Then face it as much as possible, both in yourself and in others. Investigate its roots. Trace the history and evolution of its ingredients in yourself.

Think of those you've felt especially disgusted by, and imagine taking this disgust so far that these reviled others no longer feel like people to you but only humanoid objects, polluting you and your kin, your culture, your nation. Stay with this feeling for a while, witnessing it up close. Then, breath by breath, start opening your heart to any aspects of yourself you feel disgusted by, bringing these into the depths of your being, one at a time.

Once you're at home with this practice—and it may take some time—apply it to the others for whom you not so long ago felt disgust, contempt, hatred. Humanize them, and keep humanizing them; practice developing empathy for them, until their otherness shifts into an expanded, more diverse sense of us-ness. Then how you and they differ won't make enough of a difference to exclude them from the circle of your being.

As you relate more deeply to the evil of others and the collective—and to your own potential for evil—you become capable of looking not only into it but also *through* it. You can slowly but surely infuse it with at least some degree of empathy—not empathy for its deeds, but empathy that infiltrates and cracks its dark heart, like upstart green shoots breaking open a stretch of concrete; empathy that ensures we won't respond to evil with evil.

18 BIGNESS AND BEAUTY IN THE SHADOW

OUR SHADOW DOESN'T contain just our unpleasant or far-from-flattering qualities but often also some of our finest qualities and capacities. It might seem odd that we'd conceal such things in our shadow, but we often do. One of the biggest surprises awaiting us when we explore our shadow is the possible gold there—the presence of the very best in us, out of sight but still intact, still ready to be mined. What's ennobling in us may be so hidden in our shadow that we all but forget it, reducing it to a fantasy or viewing it as something that only certain esteemed others have.

When we, as children, began developing a shadow—a storehouse for whatever in us seriously conflicted with our survival needs—not everything deposited there was necessarily the "bad," "wrong," or anti-social stuff. Some of it was our best qualities—such as our vastness of spirit, our openness to far-from-conventional realities, our true size (the fullness of who and what we really are). Not that this happened to all of us, but it did for many of us. As much as our social environment might have encouraged our full-out aliveness and the blooming of our unadulterated uniqueness, it also may have shut us down, so as to bring us more into alignment with its "civilizing" framework.

Maria was terrified of performing in front of others, even though she'd been told many times she had a lovely voice. Her throat would close up, and she would shake so badly that she often couldn't get her voice out. Her true voice—and her true size—were hidden in her shadow. As we worked together, she went back to her early years when her parents and teacher told her to just mouth the words when her little choir was performing, because her voice apparently was just too loud and penetrating. Such disapproval became the core message of her inner critic. Her work was, in part, to fully meet the little girl in her, to both love and protect that little one and safeguard her from the bullying deliveries of her inner critic. As she became more intimate with her inner child, without fusing with that little one's reality, she was able to let her own light shine more, becoming more embodied and empowered. She stepped into her true size, out of which her essential voice emerged, beautifully and fully.

Sometimes our best qualities, our deepest gifts, emerge from our shadow without any apparent catalyst or work on ourselves. When I was twenty-one, I was in a doctoral program in enzyme biochemistry, and one afternoon was doing some research in the university library. Though the science bored me, I plugged away, as I had ever since I was strongly encouraged to turn from the arts to science as a young teen. Suddenly, with no plan whatsoever to do so, I began writing poetry, scribbling with great intensity for at least an hour. I'd not written anything creative since I was a boy. I didn't stop; I didn't question what I was doing. When I was done, I went to the house I shared with three other graduate students and happily subjected them to every lurid line of what I'd written. I've been writing ever since, and I would continue doing so if no one ever read a word of mine. The writer in me has never returned to my shadow.

The more we deny or marginalize the ennobling parts of our shadow, the more we tend to project them onto others, especially seemingly heroic figures, who then reside on pedestals for us, out of reach but still available for adulation. As long as we have out-of-reach figures carrying the ennobling parts of our shadow, we don't have to face these in ourselves, which means that we don't have to assume any responsibility for having such qualities, let alone actually live in accord with them.

We can, when caught up in romantic infatuation, easily project the very best qualities in us onto the other person. How wonderful they may then seem, how gloriously alive and open, how magnificent! How could we not fall in love with such a person? But with whom exactly are we falling in love? Not the other person! Our charge, our excitation, is magnetized not only to the other person's euphorically juicy fit with our own conditioning but also to qualities in us that are still doing time in our shadow, even as they seem to emanate from the other person. Romantic infatuation may be a short-lived bubble of make-believe intimacy, but it can show us not only things such as our investment in overlooking relational red flags but also our ease in projecting onto others that which we have disowned or rejected in ourselves.

The Risk of Unearthing Our Hidden Treasures

Bringing treasures out of our shadow can feel just as risky as bringing out the less savory things we've hidden there. There's considerable hesitation and fear in fully owning the ennobling parts of our shadow because of what doing so requires of us. For example, once we recognize our capacity for being-centered love, we can't so easily settle for self-centered love or romantic entanglement.

Once our true size and gifts have been exposed, there's more that will be expected of us. Once we've shown that we can lift the whole building, who's going to take us seriously when we complain about having to lift just a few bricks? Once we've removed the lid from Pandora's golden box, our best qualities are out there for all to see. Getting them completely back in the box is then no more possible than refilling and resealing the box was for the original Pandora.

There's great value in having the gold of our shadow out in the open—and there's also great freedom in having it at our fingertips, given what it allows us to do. But this freedom is far more than mere license, far more than just indulging our preferences. How we use it is of utmost importance. When we realize right to our marrow that for every increase in freedom there's a corresponding increase in responsibility, it becomes much more difficult to engage in various freedoms without taking into account the impact our actions will have on others.

It's crucial to note that our best qualities, once out into the open, may drive other qualities—ones that aren't so esteemed—into our shadow if our early history was one of needing to suppress these "lesser" qualities. Think of children who receive support when they're brightly shining and excelling, but who receive disapproval when they express anger, hurt, and resistance. Making room for the gold in us works best when doing so isn't in opposition to making room for the iron, the coal, the dirt-stained in us.

Bring forth the gold from your shadow, but don't do so at the expense of what's not so golden! Everything in your shadow—*everything*—has value. Mine anything in your shadow deeply enough, and you'll find gems, life-giving surprises, essential clues, unsuspected riches. And all of it fundamentally is—once brought out into the conscious open—reclaimed you. Don't settle just for the gold.

19 THE SHADOW OF SHADOW WORK

I HAD MANY significant breakthroughs—emotionally, psychologically, and spiritually—in my twenties and early thirties. I felt furthered—and more than mildly inflated—by the work I'd done on myself, so that by the time I'd reached my midthirties I assumed I didn't need to do much more.

I was more vulnerable and willing to look at myself than I had been, more capable of intimate relationship, but I didn't see—or want to see—that I hadn't reached the peak. I only stood just above the base, making daytrips to the higher slopes. As important as the work was for my well-being, it was basically just preparatory work, readying me to go much deeper. I didn't recognize that the essential work we're called to do on ourselves isn't something we complete in a few years but rather a lifelong, ever-evolving adventure.

It's crucial not only to engage in the healing and awakening work that we need but also to keep a keen eye on the part of us that doesn't want to persist in doing this work, that wants to quit and coast and act as if there's nothing more to do. I let that aspect of myself usurp the throne of self for years, projecting what was still unhealed in me onto others. I turned away from the signs that I wasn't where I thought I was. This is the shadow of shadow work: acting as if we've arrived when we've done little more than start out.

I took this to another level altogether in an experimental community I began in 1986. I was unknowingly attempting to create the kind of family I didn't have as a child, one in which I wouldn't be abandoned or overpowered. I let my ambition to keep the community intact override the needs of its members, and I didn't question my decisions. I hurt others through my actions while assuming that their hurt had nothing to do with me and that their pain was necessary for their growth. My shame was deep in my shadow; I was unaware of how it ran me and how much others were impacted when I shamed them. Most of my empathy was also buried in my shadow. My grandiosity grew unchecked. I had a long way to fall.

When I was finally brought to my knees, following a horrendous, drug-induced near-death experience in 1994, the community, now a cult, ended, and I lost literally everything I had, including my sanity for several months. I was broken down to ground zero, forced to learn to bear the unbearable. No longer was I so immune; I felt not only my own wounding but also that of those I'd loved, those I'd hurt, those I'd had far too little empathy for. I was deeply humbled. My shame and remorse were excruciatingly immense—and long overdue.

I stayed sufficiently shattered to not be able to return to my old ways. I emerged from my breakdown—eventually a breakthrough—feeling a compassion I'd not known before, a depth of caring that cut through most of my remaining arrogance and sense of entitlement. The compassion, humility, and gratitude I felt formed a new foundation for me; when I strayed from it, I wasn't gone for long. I began examining my shadow more deeply, coming to understand much, much more about shame. I no longer thought of work on myself as something I'd one day complete but as a life-giving, ever-deepening exploration and evolution that I'd be involved in for life. I came to learn that authentic shadow work is a journey of endless discovery.

There's a temptation when we've been working with a particular shadow element for a while to assume that we've done enough, that we've got it sufficiently handled. For example, if we've become aware of our tendency to be defensive when our partner questions us, and more often than not can admit its presence, we might think we've worked it through. It's great that we've reached this point, but stopping here may keep us from seeing our less obvious sorts of defensiveness, such as not looking or sounding defensive while still remaining committed to being defensive. If our partner picks up on this, and we deny it—instead being subtly defensive about our alleged subtle defensiveness—we may go unquestioned, but our relationship will suffer. It will be saddled with a bit more distance and a bit less trust. We have learned a certain degree of transparency, but we confuse it with full transparency, and our partner can feel this, even if they don't say anything about it.

Another example of stopping short is that of premature forgiveness: we assume that we've forgiven someone who's wronged us when in fact we've only done so superficially. Our shadow here includes not only the payoffs we get—both internally and externally—for being somebody who can so easily forgive but also the emotions we'd rather not acknowledge, let alone express, about what was done to us. For example, if we feel hate toward the person who wronged us and don't want to acknowledge it, we can keep such hate out of sight by acting as if we've forgiven the person and moved on, perhaps giving ourselves a spiritual pat on the back for our achievement.

Our shadow often includes our investment in assuming we've done enough inner work in a particular area and therefore don't need to explore it anymore. Also, our shadow may include fearfulness regarding further exploration and perhaps also some anticipated shame regarding the possibility of failing in such exploration.

The point isn't to always keep digging away, overinvestigating our behavior and personal history, but to remain open to further deepening. We've taken a risk in beginning to work with our shadow elements, and we've done well—and it's fine to rest for a while, so long as we don't confuse our taking a break with no longer needing to do any shadow work.

The temptation to sit back, to stay put, isn't something to condemn or shame ourselves for but something to include in our adventure of awakening, beginning with exposing it and clearly admitting it.

Looking More Deeply into Our Intentionality

As we progress in working with our shadow, it becomes increasingly important that we learn to recognize the ways in which some of our intentions may be part of our shadow. What we do can appear very straightforward, but at the same time can camouflage an underlying intention. An obvious example is when we behave warmly toward someone not because we like them but because we want to increase the odds that they'll oppose an enterprise we'd like to see fail. What's in the shadows here isn't necessarily deeply hidden but nonetheless is out of plain sight.

We may have brought our vulnerability and sensitivity out of the shadows to a noticeable degree and, having begun to face the wounding that kept them in the dark, we have an increased capacity for relational intimacy. But much may be camouflaged by our newfound openness and capacity for transparency and tenderness.

In some cases, we may intentionally use such vulnerability and sensitivity not only to deepen our connections but also to manipulate those we're relating to. For example, we might intend to use our newfound capacities to draw a person into being sexual with us. We might even frame their being seduced by us as a sign of their openness, their willingness to take risks. We might seem loving and transparent in giving such "appreciation," but our ulterior motive is still very much present. We're keeping our intention in the shadows, along with our investment in it, and our apparent changes for the better (our vulnerability, especially) can very effectively mask this hidden intention.

Intention can get very subtle. We can sincerely intend to help others and yet at the same time be fueling a more submerged intention: to reap the benefits of being seen by others as someone who can really help and who wants to be of deep service to others. What's being kept in the shadows here is our acknowledgment of this decidedly unflattering intention.

The eighteenth-century English poet Alexander Pope famously said that a little learning is a dangerous thing. The same can be said about a little shadow work. If we stop short in such work, doing just enough to generate a bit more wholeness and a bit less fear, we may assume not only that we've done enough but also that we arrived somewhere we actually haven't: at an integrated state that signals real maturity. Instead, we've only gone partway up the mountain, leaving much of our shadow unexplored.

Also, we may have conceived of our shadow as a kind of storehouse with its contents spread out all over the floor, all of it equally visible once the lights go on. But some shadow elements are harder to spot than others. Disowned anger and suppressed shame are usually easy to see, especially when compared to less "solid" phenomena, such as intention and motivation.

Furthermore, some qualities can be both easy to spot and difficult to clearly see. Consider transparency—a highly valued virtue in most personal-growth circles these days. A little transparency in us—letting our inner workings show, at least to some degree—has a very different impact on others than no transparency. Showing considerable transparency can be very appealing to others, but it still can obscure or block full transparency.

When we are completely transparent, we either have no secrets or have ones that we can openly acknowledge. If we have any agenda to manipulate others, we're clearly candid about that. No hiding. No shadow. Implicit in this is consistently being our own whistle-blower. We're then an open book, at least with those we're close to, not using our transparency in the service of hidden or ulterior motives.

Recognizing What Motivates Us

Having only an intellectual grasp of deeper truths can be a dangerous thing, for this kind of understanding can be easily confused with directly experiencing these truths. What's in our shadow here is our lack of acknowledgment of our inexperience regarding such matters—and perhaps also our desire to be seen as knowing things that we don't really know. The status that may come from the apparent understanding, or ability to articulate the *theory*, of something "deep" can be quite seductive.

Recognizing what motivates us is essential if we're to cease being run by our conditioning. We can reach the point where we're able to speak about what's driving us in certain circumstances, but we may use this capacity to camouflage what's driving us at a deeper level. For example, we may give generously or be very attentive, and we may assume that we do so because we simply want to make a difference, "give back," or be of service, when in fact we're motivated by our desire to feel better about ourselves or to get a certain kind of recognition for our efforts.

In such circumstances, we must be our own whistle-blower as much as possible, and as deeply as we can, and refrain from using others for our own selfish purposes. This means doing what it takes to see such tendencies in ourselves and doing our best not to act them out.

If we conceive of our shadow as a closet, it's not a small one. It's as roomy as is needed, with the capacity to hold all that we've disowned, rejected, marginalized, or otherwise denied in ourselves, including certain intentions and motivations. When we enter the domain of our shadow, we tend to focus on what's most obvious; the foreground and bulkiest items get our attention. And this is usually fine for a while.

But eventually we need to explore our shadow more fully, checking out its nooks and crannies, its hidden shelves and cubbyholes, wearing our attentiveness like a miner's headlamp. There's a lot to see, a lot to feel, plenty to illuminate. And in such robust investigation our shadow will feel less like a closet or storage space, and more like a lost continent of ourselves, long submerged and now surfacing below a spread of moonlight.

Just because you've worked with a shadow element for a while, don't assume that you're done with it. Don't turn your back on it. It's not that there's no end to such work but that we may assume we've completed it when in fact we haven't. And we may never get completely rid of a particular shadow element—such eradication is a fantasy that populates many a mind—but we can change our relationship to it, to the point where it no longer obstructs us.

Many have come to me saying they can't believe there's more for them to face and work through in a certain area. They say that they've already done so, so much work with this area—decades of therapy, loads of spiritual practice, and so on. They're often heartlessly self-critical about the work they need to continue to do, as if they should have worked this particular issue through long ago. My initial response to them is that having an issue resurface isn't necessarily a sign of weakness or failure on their part but rather a sign that they now may be ready to face it more fully than ever before.

What's often in the shadows here is their naked shame, along with their fear that they'll never get through the issue they're presenting. Such fear is commonly accompanied by the fantasy of no longer having the aforementioned issue at all! Their challenge is not only to bring this fantasy out into the open but also to reach into the pain that's at its core and that animates it. By doing this, they learn to relate to—and explore the originating factors of—their presenting issue rather than sidestep it. They recognize that though it may to some degree still show up in them, their presenting issue doesn't have to run them. Eventually, the behaviors that characterized that issue will simply cease to arise, not because they've been repressed but because they're no longer being fueled. We have the capacity to outgrow what's unhealthy in us.

Real shadow work isn't something to dabble in, to get a certificate in after a short time of study and consideration. It's a lifelong undertaking, rich with endless discovery and deepening, an essential part of the path to full transparency and intimacy with all that we are. Eventually shadow work becomes not work but a natural aspect of living a fully human life.

PART TWO
WORKING WITH OUR
SHADOW

20 SHADOW WORK IN PRACTICE

ONCE WE REALIZE that we, like everyone else, have a shadow and don't take this as some sort of shortcoming, we're in a position to do more with our shadow than just think about it. So where to start? How do we enter the work of encountering our shadow—and its various ways of manifesting—in ways that deepen and enrich our lives?

Signs That Your Shadow Is Showing Up

Begin by identifying the signs that indicate the presence of your shadow. Bring a penetrating eye to your behaviors, especially the kind that you might describe as not really being you—behaviors that make you say, "I don't know what got into me" and other such statements suggestive of being "possessed."

Take some time to explore how any of the following signs apply to you and in which circumstances they're most likely to appear.

Reactivity. This means automatically and repeatedly acting the same way and losing ourselves in the ensuing dramatics. When we're triggered—when we have a self-righteous, disproportionate, or far-from-fitting response to something or someone—we're being reactive. Our buttons have been pushed, and we're letting our emotions have their way with us.

Reactivity is activated shadow material. The first step in handling it, once we're aware of it, is to simply admit that we're being reactive. Doing so increases the odds that we'll cease letting our reactivity remain in charge of us. When we're being reactive, what's mainly bursting out of our shadow is unresolved and unacknowledged wounding, especially that which happened in our early years.

Projection. When we (1) attribute something to another that's in us and (2) don't recognize that this something is in us, we're projecting. Projection is particularly common when it comes to qualities we dislike so much that we vehemently deny their existence in us. Think of the Cold War, in which Russia and the United States projected their worst qualities onto each other, framing each other as the villain and arming themselves to the extreme. We may also attribute something to another that's not in us but that we have a charge with, and not recognize what we're up to. An example of this is projecting the domineering mother of our childhood onto our partner during an argument, reacting to our partner as if they're indeed that parent.

Projecting a certain quality onto others doesn't necessarily mean that they don't have that quality in them, but it does mean that we may well be blinding ourselves to its existence in us. What's in our shadow here is whatever we've disowned in ourselves to such a degree that we're adamant it can't be in us.

It's worth noting that the notion of projection can also easily be misused, as when we're mired in the often erroneous belief that *whatever* bothers us in someone else is always actually in us.

Aggression. When we're being aggressive—whether we're being sarcastic, hostile, mean-spirited, or worse—we're not just angry but also on the attack. In anger, we may stay in touch with our caring for whomever we're angry at, but in aggression we've completely lost touch with that caring. Our heart is closed. *We're in the dark.* We need to learn to express anger without getting aggressive. We don't need to quench the fire of aggression but to bring some vulnerability to it, ceasing to treat the other as something to attack. That means we let our aggression shift back into clean anger—meaning anger that doesn't blame, shame, or otherwise fight dirty.

Outwardly expressed aggression—ranging from contempt to passive aggression to violence—does damage, but so too does inwardly expressed aggression, as most commonly demonstrated through the heartless shaming delivered by our inner critic when we give it free rein to take us down. In both cases, what's in our shadow are our vulnerability and softness, along with our investment in dehumanizing our target, be it another person or ourselves.

Excessive positivity. Having an exaggerated investment in being positive separates us from our shadow and its riches. When we're being so resolutely upbeat, it may seem as if we don't have a shadow and that all we have to do to thrive is stay positive. This inordinate positivity distances us from our shadow, and it also distances us from real emotional and psychological depth, tranquillizing us to varying degrees from feeling the suffering of others. What's in our shadow here are our apparently nonpositive states, especially our anger, fear, and shame.

Emotional numbness. Being significantly cut off from our emotions keeps us in the shallow end of the relational pool, "safely" removed from the pain that we associate with such emotions (such as having been rejected for crying or showing anger when we were young). When we find ourselves emotionally flat, disconnected, or numb, we have an opportunity to see our shadow in action, showing up in the form of whichever emotions are being shut down or gagged. It's very easy to normalize numbness or even to interpret it as a healthy state, a detachment indicative of spiritual advancement.

Instead of putting up with or flagellating ourselves for our numbness, we can acknowledge our numbness and start compassionately exploring it and what underlies it. What's in our shadow here are not only the emotions that we're dissociating from but also our attachment to continuing to believe that it's better to leave them as far from us as possible.

Eroticizing our unresolved wounds and unmet needs. This behavior is the result of having funneled our charge with certain situations and persons from our early years into sexual contexts. For example, if we faced heavy aggression from one parent, feeling very afraid of them, and had a resulting charge with being thus overpowered, we might later in life let this charge find some expression and release through being eroticized, by acting out unhealthy power dynamics with sexual partners. What's in our shadow here are our unresolved wounds and unmet needs, in close association with the child within us—all of the nonsexual factors that are at play in our sexuality. (For more on eroticism and the shadow, see chapter 11, as well as my books *Transformation Through Intimacy* and *To Be a Man*.)

Using pornography. Just because our culture overtolerates pornography doesn't necessarily mean that using it is a healthy practice. It's easy to eroticize our unresolved wounds and seek respite from them through sexual activity, and the use of pornography is a big part of this eroticization. The point is neither to okay pornography nor to condemn it, but to learn to *outgrow* it, so that we're available for truly healthy intimate relationships. (For more on outgrowing pornography, see my book *To Be a Man*.)

What's in our shadow here are the *nonsexual* factors that may be running our sexuality—especially the unaddressed wounding and unrequited needs from our early years, and our investment in our sexualized "solutions" to this old but still insufficiently addressed pain.

Dehumanizing others. Once we've dehumanized others, we're narrowed and diminished in our own humanity. Much of our culture is dehumanizing, as demonstrated by the reduction of others to inconveniences, mere problems, marketing icons, roadblocks to our success, and so on—and all too much of this dehumanization gets normalized. When we're reactive, projecting, aggressive, using porn, and so on, we are, to whatever degree, dehumanizing others.

What's in our shadow here are our empathy and compassion, accompanied by various payoffs for engaging in dehumanizing activity, such as our getting to stay separate from, immune to, and/ or superior to others.

Overtolerance of others' aggressive or harmful behavior. This reaction is especially easy to slip into if our early conditioning taught us that challenging others' aggressive or harmful behavior is dangerous (resulting in the loss of safety, the loss of love, or the presence of punishment). And this overtolerance is made worse when we act as if it's a virtue—especially a spiritual virtue. We often mask our fear of taking a stand with a show of care. What's in our shadow here are our anger and self-respect, along with the roots of our fear of taking firm, out-front stands.

An exaggerated need to please or to be liked. This need stems from a childhood history of things going badly when we were ourselves, but less badly when we behaved in ways that were pleasing or otherwise acceptable to those who held power over us. Wanting to be liked is rooted in wanting to be accepted; if we had an early history of not being accepted—and I speak here not only of our behavior but also of our very being—we'll attach excessive importance to being liked. What's in our shadow here is our self-acceptance, along with our anger.

Self-sabotage. This shows up as procrastination, martyrdom, settling for crumbs, and so on, in the midst of which we play victim, "trying" to make things better but only continuing to derail ourselves. When we're obstructing ourselves, it may look as if we're just being unfairly treated, as if we're a victim of forces beyond our control. The payoff is that we get to avoid taking responsibility for what we're doing to ourselves. Slipping into guilt and its self-punishing rituals is our common reaction to our self-sabotage, but such practice is just more avoidance of being accountable. What's in our shadow here is our inner child *and* our neglect of it, accompanied by our attachment to staying small, to not having to grow up. (See chapter 24 on self-sabotage.)

Refusal to say that we're sorry. When we know that we've hurt another and simply won't admit that we've done so and won't genuinely say that we're sorry, we have to harden, to cut ourselves off from our heart. Even if we somehow manage to squeeze out an admission of being sorry, it's probably voiced with minimal emotion and care so that our ego remains intact. The emotion that stands out here, regardless of its nonexpression and nonadmission, is shame.

Our refusal to say that we're sorry keeps us distanced from our shame, "protecting" us from having to directly feel it. Such shame easily slips into aggression, which allows us to harden in the face of whomever we've just hurt, perhaps even to punish them for putting us in a position in which we had to feel, however briefly, the presence of our shame. What's in our shadow here are our shame and our vulnerability, along with our investment in remaining emotionally intact.

■

Make your consideration of your shadow signs a compassionate one, especially when parts of it stir up shame in you. For each item, look deeply into what's hidden—the shadow elements—and take some time to recollect times in your life when you've engaged in such practices, whether it was an hour or thirty years ago.

Make sure that you work with this list of signs in a nonabstract way; ground your exploration physically and emotionally. Stay in touch with your body and what you're feeling. When you're looking back at what triggers you—such as another's sarcasm, their neglect, or your sense that they've not met certain standards—allow yourself to go into the bare feeling of this trigger and to stay with the feeling.

Find out and name the characteristic sensations and feelings of being triggered. Register this information not just mentally but also physically and emotionally. If your jaw tightens when you're focusing on something that gets you feeling reactive, bring your full awareness into your jaw. Without trying to untighten it, sense the various qualities of this tightening or constriction—its intensity, texture, density, sense of shape and color, emotional tone. (For more on the qualities of pain, see chapter 29.)

Carry this investigation into your shadow, identifying its elements in more and more detail, along with what first drove these into your shadow. Keep this exploration down to earth.

An example: Bob now knows that he tends to keep much of his anger in his shadow. Previously he claimed not to have anger in situations where he was actually angry—times when he showed no outward signs of anger. Much of the time, he was unaware of his anger because he couldn't feel it.

But now that he's aware of the anger stored in his shadow, he feels it and brings more awareness to it, without any pressure to give it expression. As he scans for tension in his body, he senses his anger's shape (perhaps tightly fisted), its texture (perhaps hard or rough), its density (perhaps quite thick), its coloring (probably reddish or black or both), its directionality (probably a wanting-to-thrust-forward kind of movement), and more. He also goes over his history with anger, both his own and that of significant others, viewing the choices he made regarding his anger and its expression or lack thereof. He starts to distinguish anger from aggression. And he continues to mine his shadow for more of his anger.

Soon he takes on the practice of acknowledging the presence of his anger in daily life, simply saying something such as "I'm feeling angry," "Anger's here," "I'm irritated," or just "Anger." There's no need to express it at this point; what's important is that he's starting to bring his anger out of his shadow, giving it both a caring and curious eye. He's beginning to change his relationship to it. If he persists and learns how to express it cleanly, including when it's fiery, he will have turned his anger from a jailed darkness to an outright ally.

Further Steps in Working with Your Shadow

After (1) learning to recognize your shadow, (2) meeting and illuminating what's in it, and (3) connecting the dots between your shadow's contents and your early history, you're ready for further practices, as follows.

Speaking and emoting *as* a particular shadow element. We may already *unconsciously* speak and emote from a particular part of our shadow, such as when we, relatively repressed in our anger, lash out at another. But in a suitably private setting, we can also *consciously* speak and emote as though we're actually a particular part of our shadow. Then we may still be just as loud, just as intense, *but we're operating within a predetermined context.* In so doing, we're making things much more *explicit.*

The more dramatic we are in such expression, the better; we're engaged in full-out, perhaps outrageous but nonetheless *conscious* acting. The aim here is *full* disclosure. We're deliberately giving a face to the previously faceless, a voice and emotional expression to the previously muted, an out-front presence to the previously disembodied or poorly embodied.

> **Brad** (*stomping his feet*)   I hate anyone telling me
> how to live my life! I know what the hell I want,
> and I damn well will do it, even if it upsets
> everyone! No one can stop me! No one!!

Speaking *to* a particular element of our shadow. Once we've expressed ourselves as though we were a particular part of our shadow and have done so fully, we're ready to speak *to* it—to relate *to* it. By doing so, we break our identification with it in order to stand apart from it. So if we're expressing anger, we start to view such anger from a bit of a distance, choosing to relate to it. We may still feel angry, but now we are, to a significant degree, experiencing it as an object of our awareness.

This practice can be given more depth and immediacy if we *personify* the element to which we're speaking. So if we're speaking to the anger we've kept in our shadow, we might imagine that we're addressing the angry us, either in general or at a specific age (perhaps the age at which we first started suppressing our anger).

> **Brad**   Yeah, I get it. You're super angry about
> constantly being told you can't ever do it right.
> Stupid high school teacher on your back, your
> dad shouting at you to get your act together,
> your mom nagging.

Speaking *with* a particular element of our shadow. We can have a dialogue with a particular element of our shadow, but only after having engaged in the previous two practices (speaking *as* it and speaking *to* it). Speaking with an element is usually best done by setting up two pillows (or chairs) a few feet apart and then imagining that you're sitting on one pillow (or chair) and the personified shadow element is sitting on the other. Spontaneously go back and forth physically between the two positions, speaking without any rehearsal as each one, without restraining yourself emotionally. If you feel self-conscious, be more dramatic, exaggerating your gestures and emotional tone, and move quickly—without any hesitation—when it's time to switch positions.

> **Brad** (*on pillow #1*)   No wonder you're so angry. You had plenty to be pissed off about.
>
> **Brad** (*on pillow #2*)   I'm still angry. I'm outraged! No one seems to see how competent I actually am. They keep treating me like a child.
>
> **Brad** (*on pillow #1*)   Yep, it gets maddening when they do that.
>
> **Brad** (*on pillow #2*)   I hate it. And I'm so, so tired of it. (*Tearing up.*)
>
> **Brad** (*on pillow #1*)   I wish I could have protected you from all that hassling.
>
> **Brad** (*on pillow #2*)   I just want it to stop. I wish everyone would leave me alone!
>
> **Brad** (*on pillow #1*)   Wow, I can really feel where you are in my body—my gut tenses up whenever I think someone is being critical of me.

Integration. Don't go for this practice with a particular shadow element until you've been through the preceding three practices a number of times, have become relatively comfortable in the presence of this element, and have at least some sense of *intimacy* with it. You don't have to like it, but you need at some point to compassionately hold it, like a rejected child who is finding their way into your arms. What I mean by *integration* is inclusion that's as discerning as it is deep. Being intimate with a shadow element doesn't mean that we simply tolerate its agenda and ways of acting out; we instead keep it close, keep a clear eye on it, and supply fitting boundaries for it. If we're each essentially a community of selves/parts/aspects, then we need to take good care of this community, both in group and individual contexts, relating as clearly and compassionately as possible to one and all.

■

Remember that whatever we're storing in our shadow can't help but significantly influence what we do. Keep this knowing close at hand while you work with your shadow elements.

Much of what plagues us is rooted in unattended shadow material. We may think that we're having a hard time or that our partner is making life difficult for us, and both of these things may be true to varying degrees. But the odds are that parts of our shadow are pulling plenty of the strings, reducing us to little more than puppets. Waking up to this fact can be quite a shock, at once humbling and illuminating.

Take reactivity in an intimate relationship: If we don't just act it out—reverting to the same old dramatics, always starring the righteous or apparently wronged us—but relate to it strongly enough to see it and its roots clearly, we have a chance to deepen our relationship, particularly through the very transparency and vulnerability required to openly acknowledge and expose our reactivity. In doing this, we're also exposing the shadow elements animating our reactivity.

Reactivity is a state melodramatically populated by what's in our shadow. Reactivity can provide us with the chance to become more intimate with our shadow, simply by bringing so much of it out into the open, however unskillfully. Then all we have to do is turn toward our now-exposed shadow with open eyes and adequate self-reflection.

Authentic shadow work isn't some clean-cut, antiseptic, or merely intellectual undertaking, but rather an inherently messy undertaking, as intense, unpredictable, and *alive* as birth. It eventually necessitates wholehearted entry into *everything* that we are, including what we despise about ourselves. The dirt can't be avoided, nor should it be. In fact, it needs to be appreciated and known without gloves, or else it won't become fitting soil for our emergence.

The more room we make for working with our shadow, the better.

Dear Sounds True friend,

Since 1985, Sounds True has been sharing spiritual wisdom and resources to help people live more genuine, loving, and fulfilling lives. We hope that our programs inspire and uplift you, enabling you to bring forth your unique voice and talents for the benefit of us all.

We would like to invite you to become part of our growing online community by giving you three downloadable programs—an introduction to the treasure of authors and artists available at Sounds True! To receive these gifts, just flip this card over for details, then visit us at **SoundsTrue.com/Free** and enter your email for instant access.

With love on the journey,

TAMI SIMON   Founder and Publisher, Sounds True

800.333.9185

ST330

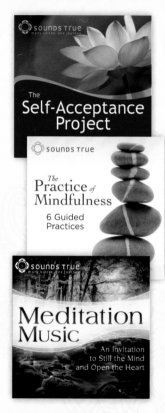

21 STRENGTHENING THE FOUNDATION FOR SHADOW WORK

WORKING WITH OUR SHADOW is a major undertaking, so the greater number of practical tools we can bring to it, the better. Four important practices for skillfully working with our shadow are being present, having healthy empathy, the practice of not-knowing, and holding space for our shadow elements.

Being Present

Being present during shadow work means providing an undistracted, here-and-now, grounded presence for encountering what we've been keeping in the dark. When we're present, caught up in neither past nor future, we're centered not by our conditioning but by embodied awareness. We don't ignore or distract ourselves from what we're feeling; we simply notice our emotional state and the shifting sensations in our body. We then naturally move from here to here, from now to now, our actions guided by the felt presence of Being.

Being present isn't about feeling good; in fact, it's not about feeling any way in particular. If we won't bring ourselves present when we're not feeling so great, then we'll likely not get very well acquainted with the part of us—housed in our shadow—that doesn't give a damn about being present.

It's not easy being present when we have trouble seeing our conditioning for what it is. Then what's mostly present is our past, with its accumulation of unresolved hurt and compensatory addictions, the roots of which remain intact in our shadow.

Being present may seem to offer a kind of immunity against suffering, a bastion of equanimity and nonattachment in the face of difficult circumstances. But being present isn't about comfort or disconnection from suffering. Rather, it's about anchoring ourselves in Being, regardless of what we're experiencing.

Being present to our shadow elements allows us to cease treating them as less than worthy of our awakened attention, so that they can be worked with, cleaned up, and integrated with the rest of our being.

HOW TO GET PRESENT—OR MORE PRESENT

The following five practices help us stabilize and deepen our capacity to be present.

Practice sensing and observing what's occurring right now, right here. Do so both outwardly and inwardly, giving what's happening your wholehearted attention. Do this periodically through each day and evening. If you feel distracted, take note of this and its pull on you. Register your emotional state and the leanings of your mind; notice the arrival and departure of your next breath—perhaps even notice your noticing. Allow yourself to settle into a sense of relaxed, undivided attentiveness.

Be self-transparent. Register and *openly* acknowledge your actual condition—inner and outer—however uncomfortable or unflattering it may be. Ways to make this more doable include not treating your pain as an enemy or problem; befriending your discomfort and resistance; not letting your inner critic have its way with you; ceasing to distract yourself from your suffering; and no longer smothering your feelings of hopelessness with hope. Here, you don't evaluate *how* you're doing with such labors but give your wholehearted attention to them, with both curiosity and courage.

Don't flee your hurt. Don't try to eradicate your hurt. Don't treat it as a problem, inconvenience, or anomaly. Don't belittle yourself for it. Rather, give it compassionate room in which to breathe and find fully alive, healing expression.

Get more embodied, grounded, down to earth. To be present doesn't mean abiding, with supposed awareness, "above" our pain and difficulties. It means being with what is. *Being present isn't an altered state*; it's our natural condition, nothing special. When we settle into it, there's a sense of being at home.

Cultivate more internal stillness. Spend some time each day sensing the space between thoughts and the space between the end of an exhalation and the very beginning of the next inhalation, and let these spaces widen, expand, open into stillness. Bring your busyness, your inner turmoil and fuss, into such stillness, bit by bit, without any pressure to alter them. Real stillness doesn't require a cessation of movement or thought but rather a *relocation* of attention to the presence of Being, the feeling of Being. You don't have to be motionless to be present. In fact, you don't have to be anything in particular. All you need is to *consciously be*, regardless of what's happening.

Having Healthy Empathy

Developing empathy for the parts of us that are in our shadow allows us to connect more deeply with them. Empathy is the capacity to resonate with another's emotional state to enough of a degree to feel it—or something closely akin to it—in ourselves. This can happen even when we don't want it to, and it also can happen when we cultivate it, deliberately putting ourselves in another's shoes.

There's unchosen empathy and there's chosen empathy.

UNCHOSEN EMPATHY

Someone chokes up telling us some news, and we, with no effort to do so, find ourselves getting teary. Their sadness becomes ours, to whatever degree. If they're fighting their sadness, trying to keep it down, we still feel it. Unchosen empathy happens both individually and collectively, and it can be very contagious.

The development of unchosen empathy begins very early; a newborn hearing another newborn's crying usually starts crying quite soon. Emotional energy has the power to cross the distance between us and another not only very quickly but also with considerable impact. Before we know it, we're plugged into another's state, viscerally connected, emotionally netted, for better or worse.

Worse? Yes—unchosen empathy, automatic and innate, can be far from a good thing, as when we're flooded or engulfed by another's emotional state. This happens with particular ease when our sense of autonomy is weak and our capacity for having healthy boundaries is hidden in our shadow.

Once we're empathically overwhelmed, we lose our sense of autonomy and our focus; we're unable to sufficiently separate ourselves from the other person. Our defining edges, our shape, our integrity as a separate person become mushy. Losing our integrity has obvious importance in relational health. Getting overly close to others, taking on too much of their feeling-state—fusing with them emotionally—gets in the way of being able to effectively relate *to* them.

CHOSEN EMPATHY

Someone starts to cry telling us some news, and we don't feel any emotional response but have the sense that such a response would be natural in this particular situation. So we imagine ourselves in their skin, in their position. Soon we start to feel something shifting in us, catalyzing a subtle melting quality, a felt warmth, that makes us feel closer to the other. Not that we always have to empathize with another, but it's good to have empathic connection as an option that we can readily access. Here, we're *choosing* to open ourselves, to allow our natural interrelatedness with another to emotionally deepen but without letting go of or weakening our boundaries.

Chosen empathy is where cognition and feeling work in healthy tandem. We know we're numbing ourselves to, say, our partner or a close friend, even though they've done nothing to upset us. Then, knowing that we can't just tell ourselves to stop being numb, we admit to ourselves that we're not being empathetic and we move toward a chosen empathy. This change takes a few seconds of thinking, of shifting perspective, and then we're imagining ourselves in the other's shoes. Even if this shift doesn't generate empathy, it gets us leaning in the direction of empathy, which enriches the relational field we share with the other.

Choosing empathy deepens our access to and engagement with what's in our shadow. For example, we've some sense of sadness in our shadow and know it; empathically contacting this sadness (as perhaps through imagining it as a hurting child) helps brings it out of the dark, closer to our heart.

KEEPING AN EMPATHIC SHIELD HANDY

I use the term *shield* rather than *boundary* or *wall* because (1) *boundary* is a very general term, lacking the hands-on feel of *shield*, and (2) *wall* is a bit too suggestive of something rigid or dense. A shield can be held, maneuvered, gripped, and positioned in different ways; it can be a living extension of us.

When we have empathy for something in our shadow but are nearing the point of getting overly absorbed or lost in it, we need to more firmly position our empathic shield—*not to block out this shadow element but to regulate how much we let it in, how much we let it affect us.*

As we feel at least some empathy for a shadow element we're facing, we have access to more data, more relevant information, regarding this element than if we were to keep our distance. At the same time, our empathic shield is in place, however thin or transparent it might be, giving us just enough separation from this shadow element to keep it in clear focus. We're close but not too close. Instead of being fused with a particular shadow element, we're choosing to be *intimate* with it. We've *expanded* our boundaries to include it rather than collapsing them in order to include it.

When both our empathy and empathic shield are functioning together optimally, we're open, receptive, and fully attentive. We make room for and register the impact that our shadow elements (and those of others) are having on us, especially emotionally. We're available but *not too available*, thanks to our empathic shield. This is empathy at its best.

The Practice of Not-Knowing

The capacity to be in—and act from—a state of *not-knowing* is very helpful in working with our shadow, providing an openness and freshness that deepens our receptivity to what's in our shadow.

What's not-knowing? First of all, it's not ignorance. Nor does it mean that we're dumbfounded, spaced-out, mentally paralyzed, or otherwise dysfunctional. Rather, when we're in a state of not-knowing we're internally open and spacious, *uncluttered by our knowledge* and not attached to any preset structuring or direction. In this state, we remain strongly embodied and well grounded, giving our wholehearted attention to whatever and whoever is before us. Not-knowing is openness free of fixation.

In not-knowing, we're simultaneously emptied of our knowledge and in touch with it. We're like a musical multi-instrumentalist improvising moment to moment with the full backup of our instrumental savvy on tap, not so much making the melody as allowing it to keep spontaneously emerging. We're alert, easy, deeply present. Our mind is clear, our heart spacious, our gut relaxed. Our outlook is ever-fresh, vividly attuned to what's before us.

Not-knowing provides fertile conditions for effectively working with what's in our shadow. With it, we're armed with openness, unobstructed presence, curiosity, and freedom from the known, neither rushing in nor keeping our distance.

CULTIVATING NOT-KNOWING

Though not-knowing is natural to us and not all that unfamiliar—as when we wordlessly resonate and interact with the radiant presence emanating through a baby's eyes—the capacity for it gets easily pushed into the background by our conditioned knowing.

Embodying our capacity for not-knowing keeps us dynamically receptive, alert to what we might otherwise overlook. Our vision is both panoramic and finely focused; our mind is unoccupied with strategies and everyday thoughts; our intuitive radar is highly attuned without our being stressed or hypervigilant.

Here are some keys to establishing and stabilizing our not-knowing while working with our shadow:

Developing a well-grounded witnessing awareness. This is the ability to consciously abide in the midst of what's going on—internally, externally, and relationally—and to name, note, and stand apart from it without dissociating from it.

Relating *to* what's happening. Instead of identifying or fusing with what's going on, or avoiding it, we choose to be in relationship to it.

Staying empathically present. This includes keeping our empathic shield in place. Without this shield, we can easily get overly absorbed in what we're facing.

Maintaining healthy detachment. We're apart but not distant, separate but not disconnected, elsewhere but not removed.

Developing more curiosity. When we're curious, we're interested—akin to children not knowing what's under the rock and keen to find out. Being curious helps keep us from being distracted by our previous knowledge.

Deepening our intimacy with the unknown. Instead of trying to answer the Big Questions, we feel into their source, opening to something more real than answers. Absolute Mystery, as always, beckons; we can't solve or explain it, but we can open ourselves to it, deepening our communion with it. While our mind is looking for explanations, our heart abides in revelation.

In not-knowing, our sense of self is significantly transparent to Being, even as we remain clearly individuated, encompassing all our qualities, including those housed in our shadow. Such individuality allows us to stand where we in essence have always stood, but *consciously*, reclaiming more and more of our true ground.

Knowledge isn't wisdom, but it can serve wisdom, especially when we've developed some intimacy with not-knowing.

Holding Space for Our Shadow Elements

"Holding space" for others usually means being present with and for them without judgment, hosting what they're doing without any interference or direction. Our role is both supportive and neutral; our attention is both spacious and focused, and we suspend our disbelief. We're not taking sides.

Imagine a dear friend who is dying and who needs no advice, and you're at their side, simply being present with them in grounded, lovingly connected silence. This epitomizes holding space at its best.

In the same spirit, consider an element in your shadow that you ordinarily feel aversion toward—hate or greed, for example—and imagine being present with this quality, holding space for it the way you'd hold space for your dear, dying friend. Instead of keeping your hate or greed in the dark, you're being a conscious container or host for it.

For example, anger arises in us along with thoughts supportive of it, quickly inflaming us with righteous indignation. By holding space for this anger, we create a bit of distance from its heated imperatives, which gives us, in just a moment or two, room to consider more options than just getting reactive with our anger. We may still express it, but the odds are that we'll do it more skillfully than if we hadn't held any space for it.

STAGES OF HOLDING SPACE

What follows is a developmental consideration of the ability to hold space. This is described in the form of four stages that we can walk ourselves through when we're setting out to consciously practice holding space for a shadow element.

1. **Passive witnessing.** In this first stage we don't interact or emotionally resonate to any significant degree with a particular shadow element, but we're simply present for it. We've expanded our boundaries enough to include it to at least some degree, even as we remain untouched. Our presence is like that of a pleasant but neutral host, a kind of spiritual innkeeper; we're detached but not too detached, keeping a consistently unobtrusive eye on what's happening.

2. **Connected witnessing.** Here we still don't interact with a particular shadow element, but we emotionally respond to it and find some connection with it. Though we don't get overly absorbed in its world, we let ourselves be affected by our encounter with it. And we still remain present, keeping a clear eye on what's happening.

3. **Intimate witnessing.** At this stage we rest at the edge of interaction, cultivating intimacy with the emotional and psychological dimensions of our shadow elements. We're very close—relationally close—to such elements and at the same time we're maintaining just enough separation to keep them in clear focus. We're both holding space and fully inhabiting it, so that we're not on the outside looking in but are *inside the inside*.

4. **Intimate witnessing and action functioning as one.** Here, we can engage a particular shadow element without any dilution of our intimate witnessing of it, and our doings spontaneously arise from our attunement to what we're facing. We have no goal here; we're free of any preset expectations as to how we should proceed. Sometimes our intention to act will remain as an intention, and other times it will shift into action. *This isn't interference but rather communion translated into life-affirming action.*

Linda is feeling a nameless anxiety and decides to hold space for it in accord with the four stages just described. She begins by simply noticing her anxiety, *passively witnessing* it while keeping her distance; she's begun to consciously contain it. Her fearfulness lessens slightly as she does so. She knows that if she doesn't maintain her vigilance, her sense of fear might overpower her. She holds steady as best she can.

Now Linda shifts from passive witnessing to *connected witnessing*. She's not only consciously containing her anxiety but is also letting herself more directly experience it. It's much more vivid now. She still has an eye on it, but she's not so removed from it. Connections between her current fearfulness and the fear she felt as a child start to become more obvious. The closer she gets to her sense of anxiety, the more clearly she sees it.

Next she moves from connected witnessing to *intimate witnessing*. She maintains her awareness as she permits herself to get up close to her anxiety. Her curiosity deepens. She's still afraid but feels less contracted. The qualities of her fearfulness become clearer, their detailing unfolding in the light of her attention.

Finally, *she allows her intimate witnessing of her anxiety to coexist with action*. She breathes deeper, remembering how she had to hold in her anger and passion when she was a child. She'd done this by tightening her tummy and breathing shallowly; her sense then was that if she didn't thus constrict herself, something awful was going to happen (her father terrifying her with his drunken raging). Now she breathes even deeper, imagining picking up the fear-frozen little girl she'd been and feeling a surge of protective energy for her. She's still witnessing her fearfulness, even as she makes fists, stomps her feet, opens her throat, and says with great passion what she hadn't dared to say way back then. Now her initial sense of anxiety has shifted into healing anger, excitement, and soon some real peace.

POSSIBLE SHADOW ELEMENTS OF HOLDING SPACE

There can be problems, though, with holding space. For example, we can "be here now" but be overly detached and therefore not sufficiently connected to the other, be that another person or a part of our shadow. Other shadow sides of holding space include the following:

Confusing being passive with being open. If holding space for something in our shadow is more comfortable for us than actually meeting it, we might slip into passivity—simply staying in a holding pattern with this shadow element, with a tacit agenda of keeping to this pattern *because of the emotional remove that such behavior promises.* We may appear open and spacious, but in fact we're not. We're attached to remaining intact, and so we keep more distance than is needed from the shadow element in question.

Excessive detachment. If we're holding space from too far away, our encounter with the other person or a shadow element will be anemic. Also, excessive or exaggerated detachment can easily masquerade as transcendence or some sort of spiritual achievement. Our underlying motivation here is to stay intact, "safely" distanced from what's before us.

Unable to stay present with strong emotions. If we shy away from, say, openly expressed grief, our holding space for such expression won't constitute an authentic openness but rather a barrier, a defense, behind which we retreat. The work needed here is to open to our own emotions, to learn how to both fully and skillfully express them and contain them, to no longer confine them to our shadow or seek a "safe" remove from them. It's helpful here to remember that our basic emotions themselves aren't negative, but what we *do* with them can be negative.

Overattaching to keeping things under control. Being overly concerned about controlling what's happening—as when what we're encountering in our shadow is emotional rawness—greatly contracts whatever space is being held, decreasing whatever safety is present.

Avoiding taking action when it's needed. Sometimes holding space isn't enough—such as when what we're facing in our shadow is crossing the line into extreme agitation, and keeping ourselves apart from this feeling only aggravates the situation. Under these conditions, we may try to just stay as we are—attached to remaining uninvolved. Perhaps we think that we shouldn't interfere, but to not step in is more harmful than staying put. For example, we're holding space for some childhood pain we've encountered in our shadow, and we're trying to keep from feeling that pain, to the point where we're basically numbing ourselves to it. What we need to do is start moving *toward* such pain, letting ourselves openly feel it and feel into the child who originally experienced it.

In the deeper stages of holding space for what's in our shadow, we're not only dynamically present but we're also able to step in, to make fuller contact. This kind of holding space is one of being decisively engaged with what we're facing; our actions may arise from a relatively still place in us, but they're allowed to arise in the spirit of compassionate activism.

Confusing being disengaged with holding space. When we truly hold space for a shadow element, we're engaged with it. We're not on the fence.

Thinking that being nonjudgmental means having no judgments. Truly holding space doesn't mean being free of judgments, since having judgments—positive or negative—comes with having a mind. Instead, it means not letting judgments get in the way. Sometimes when our presence deepens, our mind will get very quiet and be free of thoughts for a while; other times, thoughts—including judgments about what's in our shadow—will flood our mind. But there's no problem if we hold space for these mind-forms without taking them too seriously.

Confusing being selfless with being disconnected. Sometimes when we're holding space, our sense of self may itself become an object of our awareness, at least to some degree. Holding space while we're in this state can be uncommonly helpful, so long as we remain connected—including emotionally—with what we're holding space for. We can, however, be cut off from our sense of self and take this as a sign of spiritual advancement, as if we've gone beyond our ego, our "I." In such premature "transcendence," we may appear, at least to ourselves, to be selfless, when in fact we're simply disconnected, cut off from our humanity.

■

Holding space can be an entirely passive process or it can be a dynamic process out of which fitting actions emerge. In either case, it's an act of caring. We're present for what we're holding, operating through a mix of healthy detachment and compassion.

By holding space for our shadow elements, we can relate to them without identifying with any particular one, developing some degree of intimacy with all of them. We don't cultivate such intimacy from afar; we must gradually shed our craving for a remote control and get close—really close—to what's happening in our shadow, guided by our care, curiosity, and intuition. Our gaze is both wide-angled and precisely focused, zeroing in on the finest details. Nothing gets excluded. We're not only holding space but inhabiting it, consciously relating to whatever's in it, making room for all that we are.

22 AN INSIDE LOOK AT INNER CHILD WORK

SHADOW WORK and inner child work share a lot of common ground and, in fact, become much the same process when we're facing our unattended childhood programming and imprinting.

Our inner child is the expression and personification of two factors that are in close conjunction: (1) the intrinsically good qualities of early childhood and (2) our early conditioning. The aspects of such conditioning that are unresolved or hidden are part of our shadow, so working in any depth with our inner child includes, to whatever degree, working with our shadow elements. And shadow work has to include working with our inner child; after all, childhood is when most of our conditioning was originally implanted. Furthermore, sometimes our inner child itself is kept in our shadow, however partially.

The Inner Child

The concept of the inner child remains popular, having gone mainstream since the 1970s along with various approaches to inner child work. Though criticisms of such work abound (for example, the alleged blaming of our parents for our current difficulties), it's here to stay. Approaches range from simplistic advice to "just love our inner child" to nuanced, transformative exploration of the conditioning for which our inner child is but the presenting face.

So what is the inner child? First of all, it's not an entity, an indwelling being, but rather an activity, a personified, memory-saturated process, however much we might relate to it as though it's a discrete somebody, a literal child. Even so, the fact that the inner child is an interior process doesn't make it any less real or any less childlike.

The inner child's qualities include innocence, playfulness, curiosity, wonder, prerational knowing, and extreme openness, vulnerability, permeability. But it's *not* all love, light, and sweetness. The inner child's undefended openness lets in not just the good stuff but also the not-so-good stuff. After all, it has little or no capacity to protect itself, to screen what's incoming—just as we didn't in our early years. And so our inner child expresses both our essential purity *and* our original conditioning.

No wonder fairy tales, a mainstay of children's literature, are pervaded by so much dark or scary material, rich with themes of abandonment, rejection, and danger. Not that childhood is always like this, but plenty of it is, and plenty of the conditioning that then took hold of us follows us into our growing-up years, adulterating our adulthood. Furthermore, even the seemingly happiest childhoods can't escape the reality of conditioning.

The inner child is both pure and sullied—pure in the sense of primal innocence and openness, sullied in the sense of containing (and being branded by) our early woundedness and fear. That is, it's both unconditioned and conditioned. And again, *much of our inner child may be in our shadow.*

Many talk of embracing their inner child, but to truly do so is to come in intimate contact with both the life-giving and the life-negating, the light and the dark, the untampered-with and the tampered-with from our early years. Pushing away or denying the child within—as many are inclined to do, especially if they view their inner child as weak, needy, or embarrassing—just separates us from our unresolved wounding and unmet needs, leaving our conditioning intact. We thereby unknowingly let it run us from behind the scenes, however free from it we may think we are. Contacting and feeling—feeling *into*, feeling *for*, feeling *with*—our inner child brings us closer not only to who we were in our early years but also to the conditioning that got implanted in us then.

The inner child exists in all of us. We may identify with it, deny it, pamper it, blame it, abuse it, or think it's just an idea, but it's not going away. It's an essential part of us, no matter how much we push it into our shadow. To not know our inner child keeps us fragmented, emotionally impoverished, cut off from our deeper vulnerability and openness, while our original woundedness, shadow-bound, continues to direct us.

Signs That Your Inner Child Has Shown Up

Acting childishly—having tantrums and behaving egocentrically—is an obvious sign that our inner child is making itself known. Other key signs include:

Reactivity. When we're reactive—reverting to knee-jerk, emotionally disproportionate behavior—the wounded child in us is taking center stage, showing up through our speech, movements, intentions, and manner of relating. We're on autopilot and usually very resistant to admitting or being told that we're being reactive, even when we know better. The charge, or amplified excitation, that we have at such times, *originating in our early years*, is very strong and can easily override our capacity to embody a saner direction, if we let it.

One of the quickest ways to interrupt our reactivity is to admit to ourselves that the child in us has shown up. This gives us access to a perspective other than that of the child's. As we realize that the child's wounding has been triggered and has successfully enlisted our adult capacity to argue and rationalize, we begin defusing our reactivity.

Freezing. When we sense danger and an absence of safety, we're immediately mobilized to fight, flee, or freeze. A child who can't flee or fight will usually shrink into freeze mode, experiencing enough paralysis to hold very still and dissociate to varying degrees as this happens. Fear is present, but even more so is numbness. When we freeze during tense, confrontational, or strongly emotional times, this usually indicates that (1) the child in us has been activated and (2) we're caught in the same behavioral default as we were when we felt frightened or overwhelmed in our early years.

An exaggerated sense of abandonment or rejection. A sense of abandonment can start very early in life. Think of Dr. Spock–era infants left to cry alone through the evening and night because this would supposedly make them stronger, when in fact such neglect eroded their trust at a baseline level. When we drop into this mood of abandonment or rejection when we're not actually being abandoned or rejected in any significant sense, the child in us is looking through our eyes.

An overwhelming sense of existential helplessness. This sense may be characterized by us throwing up our hands in the air and sinking into a what's-the-point depressiveness when our circumstances actually aren't all *that* bad. There were times, in many cases, when we, as young children or infants, were in no-exit situations that were far from pleasant and the only solution was to mute our vital signs—not a response we chose but something that organically arose as a survival strategy. We don't fight, flee, or freeze but rather *collapse.*

Magical thinking. Magical thinking is a mode of prerational cognition in which we assume that we have—or can have—a *causal* role in events that we actually have no control over. This way of thinking is entirely natural in early childhood (think of four-year-olds assuming that they're making the sun follow them as they walk along), and it shows up in adulthood in various forms.

When we get lost in magical thinking, we've regressed to early childhood—for better, as in the creative throes of artistic passion, or for worse, as in the egocentric spirituality of those who believe that all we have to do to change our reality is think differently (as if all that a starving mother in some barren land has to do is repeat some positive affirmations about being more prosperous).

Magical thinking can also show up when we're feeling strongly overwhelmed or are unusually distraught; for example, someone close to us has suddenly died and we find ourselves imagining that if we just do certain things a particular way, that person might come back to us. Magical thinking gives us a sense of power over things over which we have no power. Think of the appeal of fairy tales to a child—tales in which a rejected or neglected child often gains the power to dramatically affect their world for the better. There's nothing wrong with magical thinking, but it's important not to let it get behind the driver's wheel.

A sudden surge of disproportionate rage or defensiveness. This kind of reaction is very common, and just as commonly it's taken to be something over which we have no control. The root of such rage or defensiveness may be shame or a sense of being shamed, or the surfacing of what couldn't be expressed in early life trauma. At these times we're blind to what's really going on; it's as if the child in us has been armed with powerful weaponry and is able to use it.

Egocentric behavior. Being egocentric is entirely natural to a young child; it's a developmental stage and may coexist with altruism. Its workings are transparent—you can see the wheels turning. The problem is when such behavior follows us into adulthood and is allowed to squat upon the throne of self. Think of those in leadership positions who are still playing "king of the castle" with serious intent. When we're busy being me-centered, seeing everything and everyone revolving or having to revolve around us, we're acting out our early childhood egocentricity—narcissism-plus.

Goalless spontaneity, wordless wonder, pure joy. These and related states can arise without any regression to childhood, but when they do, the child in us is alive and well, shining bright. We're playing like no one is watching or overseeing us. When the innocence of the child within and the awakened innocence of real maturity meet, we're truly plugged in, at home in our wholeness.

How to Work with Your Inner Child

First, get to know your inner child. Acknowledge its presence and your feelings toward it, including if such feelings are mixed, aversive, or seemingly nonexistent.

Many don't want to get close to their inner child because of painful associations they have with their early developmental years. Initially we might not feel connected to our inner child. Identifying what it is about that little one that bothers us or turns us off is an important step to take.

If, for example, your inner child is needy and you find this neediness distasteful or embarrassing, you can look back and see what your childhood neediness resulted from (such as parental neglect or mishandling of your early needs). When you recognize and *feel* this, it may catalyze enough compassion in you that you more fully accept your inner child.

What you don't like about your inner child is very likely what significant others (your parents, siblings, peers, teachers) didn't like about you when you were a child. When you realize that this dislike *originates not in you but in these others*—and also is probably a defining characteristic of your inner critic—then you can reassess whatever aversion you have to your inner child and begin responding to her or him the way you would to any shamed or otherwise beaten-down child.

Second, cultivate empathy with your inner child. It can be helpful to visualize a child other than the child you once were in clearly difficult circumstances—perhaps as your own son or daughter, or the child or grandchild of a good friend, a child you feel a natural affinity for—and then let your caring and concern for that child arise and spread through you. Once there's no doubt that you're experiencing such feelings, *immediately* transfer this focus and feeling to the child you were and are still carrying inside, as if you are caringly and protectively present with that little one. Doing this practice over and over will help bring you closer to your inner child and its reality, so that its pain—your pain—becomes something not to avoid or distract yourself from but to approach, step by consciously compassionate step.

This is regression, and it's more than regression. You're going back in time, especially emotionally, and you're also bringing your current presence, your conscious grownupness, into that felt past and its defining memories. You're both experiencing the feelings, expressed and unexpressed, of your inner child and holding them without getting lost in them—like a good parent. You're entering a lucid empathy, emotionally resonating with the child in you while at the same time *not identifying* with that one. This empathy allows you to not only feel your inner child but to also take good care of him or her.

Third, commit to your inner child. Remember the child within daily, keeping in *emotionally alive* contact with her or him. It's as if you're driving the car, maintaining enough focus to drive well, while that child is safely present in the backseat, feeling your trustworthy, caring presence while it plays, bearing no responsibility for making sure the car stays on the road or that you're in a good mood. He or she gets to be a child, a loved and protected child, at ease in the presence of a conscious, well-embodied parent.

The more we can access and live this state, the more deeply and effectively we can encounter and work with our early conditioning. We can become a safe space, a conducive environment in which our original wounding, primal imprints, default behaviors, and core programming can be more and more fully exposed and worked with, until they no longer drive us.

Then we realize that our inner child is not the problem; what really matters is the kind of relationship we develop and maintain with our inner child. If we're truly close to that little one, that exquisitely tender locus of unadulterated vulnerability and prerational openness and wonder, we're in a position to not only hold our woundedness and early conditioning but also to be with it in ways that heal and awaken us.

Fourth, continue both to love and protect your inner child. Once we see our inner child and its dynamics clearly, and our empathy for them thrives, it's second nature both to bring our inner child fully into our heart and to protect him or her, especially in ways that he or she wasn't but needed to be in our early years. The more room we make for our inner child without identifying or fusing with her or him, the more we thrive, generating an environment in which the very deepest work can be done, work that makes us fully human.

About protecting our inner child: It's important to be far more of a guardian than a guard. It's easy to slip into overprotecting our inner child, making too much out of certain things that bother him or her, such as perceived slights that have no real substance. Our inner child doesn't need to be housed in a fortress. Exaggerated protectiveness—and its attending rationalizations—often arise when we're unknowingly fused with our inner child (such as in times of reactivity).

Foundational Daily Practices

Doing the following two practices will reinforce the preceding ways of working with your inner child. Once these practices feel natural, you don't need to do them as often, but until then it's wise to fully give yourself to them daily.

PRACTICE   Connecting with Your Inner Child

Early each morning and right before bedtime, while comfortably lying down or sitting, attune to your inner child, making contact with that very young, tender, vulnerable part of yourself, doing so with as much care and undivided attention as you can. Sense where you feel your inner child in your body and place your hands there; if you can't sense this, place one hand on your heart and the other on your belly. Let your breathing be easy, keeping your belly soft. Keep some attention in your hands as you do this.

After several minutes, say in your own words something along the lines of "I unconditionally love, accept, and support this little one who assumed he or she wasn't worthy of [*here, put in whatever fit your early childhood*]." You might follow "wasn't worthy of" with "being loved," "being protected," or "being seen"—whatever expression feels most fitting, whatever expression emotionally resonates with you. Imagine that you're holding the child very closely as you say this. And say it at least three or four times, in a soft voice, feeling each word. You can keep holding your hands on your body as you do this, or you may shift to holding a small pillow, holding it as you would a very young child.

PRACTICE "I See You"

During the day or when you wake at night, whenever you feel your inner child's presence in the form of fearfulness, contraction, numbness, fogginess, disorientation, voicelessness, and so on, say, "I see you." You can say this silently, or you can say it softly, but do say it. You are, however slightly, acknowledging the child's presence and stepping into relationship with that little one. Before, you may have been identified with the child, taking its fearfulness as yours, or you may have been cut off from the child, but now you're in contact.

After you've said "I see you" once or twice, take a couple of deep breaths, exhaling slowly and fully, saying to yourself, "Soft belly," letting your gut loosen, relax, and become more spacious. Sense yourself not as your inner child but as a caring parent who is committed to both loving and protecting their child. Place your hand or hands where you sense your inner child showing up in your body, and say, "I see you. I understand why you feel this way, and I've got your back. I'll take care of you, and I'll take care of what's happening." Or something along these lines—whatever helps give you the sense of seeing, loving, and taking good care of the child in you.

In this practice, you're not bypassing or otherwise overlooking the child's distress or pain, nor are you shaming him or her for feeling or acting a certain way. And you're not denying the child's distress or pain by saying that it's okay, that things will be fine, and so on, because the child won't believe it and won't be able to rest in full trust. You're simply settling into love, turning toward your inner child, scooping him or her up into your lovingly protective arms, reconnecting.

Whatever we do with our inner child, it's not going away. Nor should it. It's not in the way of our maturation. Loving that part of us—not as an abstraction but as a living reality—keeps us grounded in our humanity, as does taking good care of him or her. This is a key part of being wise stewards of all that we are, choosing connection with rather than dissociation from our various elements.

Cultivating a full-hearted relationship with our inner child is one of the very best things we can do for ourselves. It also greatly deepens our capacity to be in truly healthy relationships. We don't outgrow our child within but instead outgrow our dysfunctional ways of being with that little one. Our ongoing intimacy with our inner child is a gift to one and all.

23 DETHRONING OUR INNER CRITIC

YOUNG CHILDREN, so very vulnerable and impressionable, are sponges for the input of their environment, healthy and unhealthy alike; it all gets absorbed and stored in various ways and places. Our inner child can't help but reflect this. The heartlessly shaming aspects of such input soon get channeled into our inner critic, which basically bullies the child in us, however quietly, including into our adulthood.

Our inner critic's messages might be out in the open, but its roots are often largely in our shadow. If we're fused with our inner child, we'll take what our inner critic is saying as unquestioned truth, not even recognizing at such times that we have an inner critic. Waking up to this—and to the origins and anatomy of our inner critic—is essential for effective shadow work.

It's also essential to be able to gaze with at least some compassion upon whatever we don't feel so good about in ourselves, including what we may uncover while we're working with our shadow. To embody a fuller sense of self-acceptance, we need to face our inner critic and break its grip on us.

The Truth about Our Inner Critic

Our inner critic is heartless self-shaming and self-bullying in action. Regardless of how "adult" or rational its criticisms may seem to be—especially to the child in us—they're not in our best interests.

We may conceive of our inner critic as a thing or an indwelling entity, but it's actually an activity, a process, ready to flare up when we're in a vulnerable position, nailing or bombarding us with *should* after *should*, spewing forth negative self-appraisal, cutting us down to size.

Shame is the emotion at the core of the inner critic. Healthy shame triggers and is triggered by our conscience, but unhealthy shame, toxic shame, triggers and is triggered by our inner critic. For all too many of us, our inner critic masquerades as our conscience.

Our inner critic, however soft-spoken, is aggressive. As described in the anger chapter, anger turns to aggression when we stop having compassion toward the subject of our anger and shift to simply being on the attack—just as does our inner critic.

The Relationship Between the Inner Critic and Inner Child

We tend to regress into a childlike state before our inner critic when we don't see the critic for what it is. And we all have that child in us, no matter what our age, no matter how adult we may seem. When we fuse or identify with the child within, our inner critic holds the power, talking to us as though we're but a child (or an incompetent somebody). But our inner critic doesn't hold the power in any innate sense. *We* are giving it the power, the *authority*, to shame us, to degrade us for not making the grade.

We often look at the child in us through the eyes of our inner critic. So if the child in us is shy, awkward, hurting, or dysfunctional, we might look upon that little one with a sense of embarrassment or even revulsion, perhaps thinking, "I shouldn't be like that. I'm an adult. I've worked on myself. How can I regress like that?" But this kind of thinking just provides fuel for our inner critic, so that it can righteously proclaim things such as "Look at you! You're failing. You're weak. Here you go again. You're pathetic." And on it goes—the familiar litany of put-downs, making the case for us not being enough.

The impression we may get when our inner critic is speaking with such certainty and authority is that it must be a valuable voice, a wise, parental one, perhaps even one that has our best interests at heart. But one of its defining characteristics is that it has no heart. As we work to cease identifying with our inner critic and being a child before it, we learn something valuable: if we hear an internal voice that lacks compassion, lacks heart, we need not take its contents seriously.

As we acknowledge and observe our inner critic and move *away* from it, we need at the same time to move *toward* the child in us. Doing so brings out in us a sense of increased protectiveness of the child within, so that we're both loving that little one and keeping him or her safe. Once we sense the dynamic between our inner critic and our inner child, seeing that it's usually nothing but a shame-centered dramatization of the bully and the bullied, healing can begin. At such times, our inner critic retreats to the back bleachers of our psyche, perhaps so far away that we can no longer hear it. It no longer has our ear. We're taking the much-needed step of getting *in between* our inner critic and inner child, keeping the boundary between them intact.

Working with Your Inner Critic

We may think how great it would be to get rid of our inner critic, but we can no more completely eliminate it than we can completely eliminate our judging mind. What we *can* do is start changing how we relate *to* our inner critic. Once we change that relationship, bringing our inner critic's origins out of our shadow, and we cease responding to it as if we're a helpless child, the critic loses its power over us, eventually manifesting as no more than occasional background noise.

Think of your inner critic as a mental mosquito. When we stop giving away our power to our inner critic, it downsizes into not much more than a mosquito, buzzing around on the outskirts of our mind, almost out of hearing, unable to mess with us, unable to shame us, at most being a bit annoying.

When your inner critic shows up, it's immediately helpful to name it by saying something such as "Inner critic" or "My inner critic is here." Keep it simple. It may be even more helpful if you already have a name for your inner critic—a name that really fits for you (such as "the judge" or "the inquisitor"). Then you can say this name, out loud if possible, as if identifying an intruder or trespasser.

PRACTICE

Here is a sequential practice to use when you find yourself holed up in your "headquarters," with your inner critic whispering or shouting in your ear, and you know that you need to shift without delay to a more life-giving stance.

1. Name your inner critic: "Here's _____." Repeat this phrase, a touch louder.

2. Immediately shift your awareness from what your inner critic is saying to whatever sensations you're feeling in your body. In doing this, you're shifting the focus of your attention from cognition to sensation, giving you some needed distance from your inner critic's pronouncements. It also gives you more space to observe the actual energy and feeling of your inner critic as opposed to its contents and messages.

3. Direct your full attention to your chest, breathing deeply into it, and also soften your belly. Count at least ten breaths, counting at the end of each exhale; if you forget where you are, start at one again. If you remain agitated, count to ten again.

4. Now direct your awareness to the child in you, feeling into and feeling for that one, perhaps also visualizing her or him so as to make the connection more palpable.

5. Breathe your inner child into your heart, and also breathe more presence into the space you're making for that one. Do not let your thoughts convince you to do otherwise—as in "This is silly. I shouldn't be doing this." Just simply be with this step. This causes a softening and opening—your heart, shoulders, face, and whole body softening, easing, settling.

6. Have a sense of standing *between* your inner critic and inner child, with your back to the critic, so that the child isn't subjected or answerable to your inner critic. Then imagine picking up that little one, holding him or her close with one hand. Turn to face the critic, holding out your other hand, palm facing outward as if to forcefully say, "Stop!" You're generating both a field of caring and a field of protection, safety, guardianship for your inner child.

This practice creates a feeling of reclaiming and taking good care of something that we might think we should have outgrown but that's actually with us right through our entire lives—our innocence, our vulnerability, our prerational self.

Deepening Our Self-Acceptance Disempowers Our Inner Critic

There are painful, dark, embarrassing things in each of us—qualities we can easily disown, reject, or deny. But when we move toward these things, approaching them with both care and curiosity, there's a sense of them leaving our shadow, each shifting from being a disowned or rejected *it* to a reclaimed *me*. Through such radical self-acceptance, we become more whole. We can even open our heart to our own closed-heartedness by acknowledging to ourselves (and maybe to others close to us) that we're currently closed-hearted, admitting this without self-shaming and without giving our inner critic a green light.

Instead of perpetuating our self-shaming—and reinforcing our inner critic—by rejecting and pulling away from the parts of us that are seemingly messed up, we can turn our undivided attention *toward* them. When we do so, our heart begins going out to and including these parts, because we can sense our inner child in them somewhere behind the scenes, wounded and unable to deal with the wound.

Real self-acceptance isn't about tolerating or overlooking our bad behavior but rather bringing into our heart the part of us that's behind such behavior. The process here is akin to going to a frightened child and being a compassionate space for them, holding them close—not telling them that everything's going to be okay or that there's nothing wrong but just being with them, presence to presence, saying only what's necessary.

It's perhaps most difficult to step back from our inner critic's content when we know we've done some bad things—really hurt others, been selfish, cheated, lied, broken the law, and so on—and hence feel deserving of being shamed, even toxically shamed. So we bare ourselves for our inner critic's beating. But such self-battering does us no good and, in fact, prevents our healing.

Imagine that a dear friend has come to you and confessed something awful they've done. You don't condone it but at the same time you don't condemn *them*. You may feel disturbed, but you don't abandon your compassion. In so many words, you say to your friend, "Yes, you really messed up. You did some harm. It's good that you feel shame about this, but instead of putting all your energy into beating yourself up, make amends, clean it up. Feel your remorse but don't keep putting yourself down. For when you do, you're in no position to clean things up." Now imagine that this dear friend is none other than you.

You could have responded to your friend by attacking them, degrading them, condemning them. We can take a particular bad behavior—in others or in ourselves—and approach it with compassion, however fierce, or we can approach it with a stony heart. We can be a caring parent to ourselves when we've slipped, allowing our shame to fuel our conscience, or we can be an abusive parent, employing our shame as a bludgeon, a whip, a crippler. It's in our best interests to disarm our inner critic.

Our inner critic certainly can sound very convincing, but once we realize that it doesn't really care about us, we're on track to unseat it. The more that we understand its nature and recognize it when it takes center stage, the more easily we can say no to it and withdraw our attention from its pronouncements and shaming. In changing our view of it, we remove ourselves from its sway; we're no longer a child submissively responding to a difficult parent. Instead, we're simply an authentic grown-up relating skillfully to an aspect of ourselves that isn't so healthy. To thus orient ourselves is a matter of learning to directly relate to the not-so-healthy qualities in us instead of letting them overrun or bully us, or by trying to keep them out of sight. The point is to not let your inner critic run the show. And don't allow your inner critic to evaluate how you're doing with dethroning it!

To reduce our inner critic to its proper size we need to have a clear sense of its origins, our history with it. Does it sound like one parent or the other, or a composite of both? Or an older sibling who was harsh or cruel? A teacher? Schoolmates who bullied us or put us down? We need to get a sense of who our inner critic takes after and to understand that our inner critic is a complex activity within us, ready to flare up when current conditions sufficiently mimic the original conditions that spawned our self-shaming tendencies.

If, for example, we were overwhelmed by an angry parent who slam-shamed us, part of our work is to get in touch with the anger we had to repress in order to survive that parent's rages. If we have our anger on tap, we can say an effective no to our inner critic (which is also a no-longer-buried no to what our angry, shaming parent did to us). But if we don't have our anger on tap, our no will be either non-existent or tentative.

As we get a clearer sense of our inner critic's anatomy, we can start to talk *to* our inner critic. An effective way to do this is to set up two chairs facing each other, imagining that our inner critic sits in one chair and we sit across from it in the other chair; we physically go back and forth between the two, speaking as each, engaging in spontaneous dialogue. Initially in this scenario, people will often speak in a tiny or weak voice to their inner critic, but with proper encouragement (from a therapist or someone close to them) they will eventually start to speak more from their guts. They will take firmer stands, saying "No!" or "Stop!" with increasingly adult firmness. As they do, their inner critic usually becomes weaker when they switch chairs and speak as it. Then they start to realize, in so many words, "My god, it's big and scary and seems so right, but only because I give it *my* power, *my* attention. So now I'm going to starve it. I'm going to withdraw my attention and my energy from it. I won't make the child in me face it. *I* will!"

■

We often conceive of our emotions as indwelling masses—*things* within that we can just simply get out of our system, things to merely vent or discharge. Not true! Emotion isn't a thing but a process. And emotion isn't just feeling; it's feeling, cognition, social factors, and conditioning all in dynamic interplay. Our inner critic is a kind of fluid conglomerate too. There's feeling in it and thinking too, plus a load of conditioning.

We can't empty ourselves of our inner critic, because it's not a something that can be discharged or evacuated from us. But we can break our identification with it. We can cease placing our inner child in the sights of our inner critic, and instead of letting our inner critic examine and cross-examine us, we examine it. Then we can live without our inner critic having any control over us.

24 SELF-SABOTAGE UNCOVERED

ACCOMPANYING OUR INNER CHILD and inner critic is our inner saboteur, which is the part of us that, to our own detriment, still is mechanically acting out against whatever had power over us as a child. The motivational dynamics of our inner saboteur all too often remain unexamined in our shadow. Going ahead with shadow work when we haven't yet uncovered our inner saboteur cripples such work.

All of us have a capacity for self-sabotage. This tendency to obstruct or double-cross ourselves is generally viewed as something bad or rather pitiful, something that must be overcome through an ambitious flurry of positive thinking or by just trying harder. However, our inner saboteur isn't something to reject or send to rehab but rather to look into deeply, until we're able to recognize its origins, its structure, and what's driving it—and what it's *really* calling out for.

Just like our inner child and inner critic, our inner saboteur isn't an entity or thing but a process, an *activity*. We're not born with it, but once our inner critic starts to take root, usually sometime in our second or third year, our self-sabotaging tendency soon follows. Whatever its surface presentation—procrastination, unhealthy reshuffling of priorities, martyrdom, settling for crumbs—self-sabotage will remain far from uprooted if we do no more than try to outwrestle its exterior, overfocusing on its behaviors. It is immune to persuasion and self-help pep talks, however much it might secretly feed on the attention. Well-meaning suggestions, laden with common sense, as how best to proceed may garner an apparent yes or sign of agreement from us but do nothing to impact the underlying no of our self-sabotage—a no that, behind the scenes, upstages the agenda of our presenting yes.

The self-sabotaging capacity in us is mostly hidden from view, stationed in our shadow. What does show of it is the knowledge—especially the *after-the-fact* knowledge—that we've somehow gotten in our own way and have undercut or undermined ourselves in a particular endeavor, shooting ourselves in the proverbial foot. Ouch! Why we did so will remain a mystery to us until we do more with our inner saboteur than just view it as something perverse or unfortunate in us, something that poor us is afflicted with.

Does the saboteur within betray us? No, though we may view what it does as betrayal. It's more accurate to say that we betray ourselves when we, in so many words, hold our inner saboteur accountable for some failure on our part—as in, "I couldn't help myself" or "I don't know what got into me." Because when we don't bring out of our shadow what's animating our capacity for self-sabotage, we set ourselves up for more failure. And the payoff? We get to play victim to a relatively convincing degree, beset as we *apparently* are by forces over which we have no control. We may make a show of saying that we should have some control here, shaming ourselves for not doing better, while also making a more understated show of not really having such control, thereby getting to sidestep real responsibility.

Jim had been dreaming of his own startup company to manufacture his invention, which had the potential to go big time. He filled notebooks with his plans, gathered the forms to fill out for patents, talked endlessly to friends and his partner about the whole process, and even made a small prototype. But he fell short of taking the necessary first steps, such as seeing a lawyer and filing the patent forms that would allow him to actually begin producing his product. He kept meaning to do these things, but things just got so busy, he told himself, plus he didn't have enough energy, he made sure to add. The excuses piled up, taking up more and more space. He was really frustrated, knowing what a service his invention would be and that it would allow him to finally make enough money to retire. "It's so hard to get this damn thing going!" he complained. "I really want to have it all come together, but life just keeps getting in my way."

When we're caught in self-sabotage, we, like Jim, avoid being accountable for what we're actually up to. Our only requirement is that we beat ourselves up to at least some extent while we're successfully failing at doing something that we know is right for us. So we let ourselves slip into guilt and its self-punishing rituals. The guiltier we feel, the more likely we'll continue to fall short, bumping into ourselves enough to slow to a stumble, stranded from compassion for ourselves. Furthermore, *we get to stay small*, pulled back into being the child who won't give up on getting something that's not available or not available enough, but who goes about it—in conjunction with adult resignation—in ways that obstruct us.

If, for example, we're overweight and don't feel good about it, and at the same time are busy doing some serious comfort eating, we may indulge in beating ourselves up. Then, having absorbed the blows, we reward ourselves with more eating (and, feeling bad again, reach for more food to make us feel better). We might even feel a sense of justification in so doing—after all, we did take a beating, didn't we?—simultaneously numbing and shaming ourselves until we're exhausted from trying to *should* our way out of our bind.

In such an endarkened and vicious circle, we remain blind to the roots of our bind.

The Key Elements of Self-Sabotage

Our self-sabotaging tendency is fundamentally a *combination* of three coexisting factors: (1) significant neglect of our inner child's core needs, (2) overriding this neglect with what we think we *should* be doing, and (3) rationalization.

1. **Significant neglect of our inner child's core needs.** *This is the underlying layer of self-sabotage.* Such neglect reactivates our original longing to be seen, heard, felt, openly loved, given wholehearted attention—whatever was absent or in insufficient supply in our early years. The greater our aversion to taking care of these needs—bringing them out of our shadow—the greater the impact such unattended

longing will have, regardless of our distance from it. Consider the image of tiny fists pounding against the inside of our chest, muffled but insistent.

2. **Overriding this neglect with what we think we *should* be doing.** This behavior keeps us oblivious to the core needs underlying it. So often we try to do the "right" thing but fall short because in our very trying we're divided, usually with the part of us that doesn't want to proceed not getting a conscious say in what's going to happen, but nonetheless still having a considerable impact on what occurs. The part that *doesn't* want to proceed with what we think should be done is the neglected child within. If we do go ahead with what we think needs doing, we remove our focus from the child, not realizing that we're doing so. *What's self-sabotage for the adult is self-survival for the child.* "I am going on a super-healthy diet!" declares the "adult"—but the neglected inner child who's still hungry for love doesn't want to.

3. **Rationalization.** When rationalization gets hooked up with the internalized neglect that's being registered, we may then "decide"—quite automatically—to take steps that obstruct, derail, or otherwise sabotage us in a particular venture while supporting this decision with "adult" justifications. Then the eating of the otherwise off-limits cookies is conveniently legitimized for at least the time needed to get them in our mouth. "I deserve a treat after a hard day today! I can go back to the diet tomorrow."

This unconscious coalition of rationalization and internalized neglect is activated to divert us from what we think we *should* be doing—not eating the cookies—in an effort, however misguided, to bring some attention to what's being ignored: *our original pain.*

But this redirection of focus fails, *as the attention we truly long for falls on our self-defeating behavior rather than on our core pain.* We then lose ourselves in guilt, beating ourselves up for our "badness" and lack of maturity, and our deepest needs remain in the dark. How sad this is, for though we're close to our core pain, we're also cut off from it, absorbed in the dramatics of a *secondary* suffering, namely that of being "bad" or "a failure," a suffering overseen and directed by our inner critic.

Distinguishing Our Inner Saboteur from Our Inner Critic

Our inner saboteur is often confused with our inner critic, our internalized, shame-ridden, heartlessly negative self-appraisal. The differences are considerable:

- Our inner critic is an overseer; our inner saboteur is an undercover agent.

- Our inner critic is a bully; our inner saboteur is a detouring presence.

- Our inner critic undermines our sense of self; our inner saboteur undermines our direction.

- Our inner critic is a repetitively flattening message; our inner saboteur is a repetitively flattening action.

- Our inner critic shames us; our inner saboteur sets us up for shaming.

- Our inner critic is a toxic, abusive parent; our inner saboteur is a rebellious, hurt child calling the shots and disguising that by using rational, adult language.

Playing the Martyr Card

Let's consider a common form of self-sabotage: martyrdom. In relational conflicts the statement "Don't be such a martyr!" or something similar is sometimes heard, directed at the partner who is clearly being more self-sacrificing, perhaps working very hard—too hard—at giving. If this giving is essential, as in child care, then the one being called a martyr can trot out this indisputable fact as a kind of passive ammunition, which ordinarily further upsets the other, who can't argue with this fact but can argue with its being brought forth in their "dialogue." (And being accused of being a martyr doesn't necessarily mean that one is actually being a martyr.)

Those who most commonly slip into playing the martyr usually have endured childhoods in which they were neglected, overlooked, seen not for who they were but for who they were expected to be. They ached to be seen and given to, and perhaps seemingly gave up on this longing. But it didn't go away as they grew into adulthood. Instead, it simply remained in their shadow while they continued to put others' needs ahead of their own, as if there was nothing else they could do.

Part of being conditioned to be a martyr is refusing to openly ask for help—acting as if we just *can't*—especially when it's *really* needed, all the while scoring internal goodness points (and probably also some degree of imagined parental approval) for being *so there* for others in need. The trouble is, these points don't really make a difference other than to subtly elevate one's largely unseen suffering—the very suffering that reinforces the sense of sacrificing oneself to be the good child, the one who adapted to far-from-healthy parental expectations long ago.

Playing the martyr features negative self-sacrifice along with an attachment, which is shadow-bound, to perpetuating this self-sacrifice. Yes, some undeniable good is usually being done—things are on time, the kids are getting plenty of care, tasks are getting done, no matter how exhausted one may be—but the wounded child within the one who is absorbed in martyrdom continues to be neglected, relegated to the background, as if everyone else matters more.

When we act in a martyred manner, giving up our true needs for the needs of others, we tend to react as if we're oppressed, clinging to our sense of being a victim, burdened by our obligations. We're emotionally fused with the child within, even as we busy ourselves trying to parent others. In such fusion, we don't see the child—we're in too close to have any focus—but we feel that little one. His or her neglected needs and absence of self-worth gnaw at us, sabotaging other needs that we deem more important. When we wake up to this dynamic, we embrace rather than fuse with the child within, taking better and better care of that one's unattended needs—our real needs.

Trying and Self-Sabotage

If we're going ahead with a certain endeavor and are cut off from or otherwise oblivious to our inner child as we do so, that child may act out enough to snare our attention, including interrupting or derailing what we're attempting to do. There's no deliberation in this, just raw, desperate need taking over, amped up with supportive rationalizations and related self-talk.

The stop-neglecting-me desire that's going on behind the scenes and the desire to proceed with our project are two quite different forces, far more oppositional than symbiotic or cooperative. These competing desires set up an internal conflict that can knock us off track, leaving us scratching our heads, wondering how this could have happened.

These conflicting forces and their interplay are eloquently encapsulated in the earnest affirmation "I'm trying." One part of us, out front and seemingly sincere, is doing "it" while the other part, hidden and seemingly not representative of us, has no interest in doing "it" and in fact probably has some investment in "it" not happening or failing. To try is not to do. If I tell you to try to pick up the spoon in front of you and you do so, I'll say, "I didn't ask you to pick up the spoon, but to *try* to pick it up." As such, *trying is self-sabotaging effort.* It may sound good, sound sincere, but it's *divided*, at war with itself.

Trying invites and expresses self-sabotage. All the ingredients are there. Something in us is getting overridden in our trying, being left in the dust or shadows as we proceed. Think of New Year's resolutions: what's gung-ho in us about these resolutions ("I'm really going to try to get to the gym a lot more often this year!") obscures what's not gung-ho in us about such enthused ambition ("I hate to exercise!"), so that we're pushing ahead like a divided nation, with one part imposing its will on the other, all but oblivious to the insurrection it's fueling.

The far-from-direct aspect of "I'm trying" usually resides out of our usual sight; its intention to thwart our progress is housed in the more distant recesses in our shadow. Even more removed from our awareness are the origins of this intention: neglected or otherwise mishandled needs of our young selves.

Between intention and action there's a gap. *Self-sabotage mires us in this gap*, destabilizing our footing and rendering us myopic, leaving our better intentions in a confusing mix with our less-than-healthy intentions, flailing about. It's in this very flailing that we lose our way, swamped by conflicting information. It's as if we're suddenly reading three very different newspapers simultaneously, and our ability to discern between them is all but gone.

Seeing the wreckage wreaked by our self-sabotage can be quite mortifying. When such shame kicks in, our tendency is to turn away from it, to avoid it, to seek less shame-polluted territories. But when we're not so quick to spurn the shame of having sabotaged ourselves, we have more of a chance to see our internal saboteur up close. Unveil our inner saboteur and strip it of its rationalizing, and what's left? A child yearning to be seen and felt, to be freely given unconditional attention and care. Becoming intimate with our inner saboteur means directly feeling what's childlike in it, attuning to that child and the key factors that shaped it. Without such focus, the efforts of that child to get our attention may submerge, sinking back into the shadows, or they may fester into attention-snaring behaviors that block or otherwise obstruct our path.

How to Work with Self-Sabotage

What follows are the five steps essential to working effectively with our inner saboteur.

1. **Be at home with inner child work.** (See chapter 22.)

2. **Be at home with inner critic work.** (See chapter 23.)

3. **Identify your survival behaviors.** Develop the ability to name them as they arise and the ability to relate *to* them, so that when they show up, you don't lose yourself in them.

4. **Recognize the voice of rationalization in yourself.** Get familiar not just with its grammar and content but also its tone, its underlying agendas, its message, its broadcasting locales or lack thereof in your body.

5. **Put it all together:**
   a. Sense the presence of your inner saboteur. You'll notice an internal conflict about taking a certain direction and feel a pull to not do what you think is the best thing to do. You'll also notice that you're rationalizing this pull.
   b. Name it. You might say something such as "Self-sabotage is here."
   c. Name its three key elements and attune to each one:
   The neglected child: what basic feelings are arising; what primary/core needs are present.
   "Adult" activity: what you think you should be doing; what's being done to avoid or override your neglect of your primary/core needs.
   Rationalization: what's being said to support the neglected child's victory over the agenda of the "adult."
   d. Identify and attend to your primary needs without bypassing your awareness of your secondary needs. Connect with your real hunger without losing sight of your appetite for the cookies. Once you're in touch with that original hunger, your pull to the cookies will lessen.
   e. Learn how to operate from already-present, innate wholeness. Acting from an undivided place, responding from your innate wholeness, means making decisions not from only part of yourself but from your core of self.

■

Self-sabotage keeps us small, partial, divided; we get in our own way despite our efforts to proceed. The child within us, neglected in our pursuit of a particular something, is, however indirectly, calling for us.

To not heed that call, that cry, is to increase the odds that we'll soon end up in the wreckage of self-sabotage.

Our common response to self-sabotage is that we don't know how this could happen to us—after all, we had good intentions, we're doing our best; we have alibi after alibi. Instead, an uncommon response is needed: recognizing and turning toward our inner saboteur, illuminating it until we see its fundamental components. Getting to know our inner saboteur really well is an essential step in maturing. Without such knowing—and the uncovering implicit in it—our shadow work will remain in the shallows. Becoming aware of the inner workings of our self-sabotage deepens our capacity to work with our shadow.

25 DREAMS
Private Shadow Theater

DREAMS ARE THE ORIGINAL home movies—self-made, self-revealing private motion (and *e-motion*) pictures edited by our conditioning and broadcast to an audience of one, who is not just a witness but also usually up on center stage. Our dreaming consciousness is astonishingly creative and improvisational, fleshing out our shadow elements in instantly populated dramas that hold our attention. Dreams are private shadow theater.

Our shadow elements don't sit quietly in the dark, not making a fuss—like "bad" children sent to their rooms. Rather, they find outlets and expression in our dreams, however indirectly. Many of the characters in our dreams *are shadow parts cast in human or nonhuman form*. For example, our disowned power might show up in a dream as a frightening carnivore. Our shadow not only manifests in multiple forms in our dreams but also plays a central role in the genesis of our dreams.

Dreams often dramatize conflicts we're having, difficult decisions, or relationship and work challenges. They make explicit through such engrossing drama what may not be so obvious while we're in the waking state. Our shadow elements are dramatized through form and feeling in our dreams, giving us the opportunity to see through them, to relate to them in ways that can help further and deepen us.

Beginning to Work with Your Dreams

Think of your dreams as short stories in which everything matters and everything has its place, including the kind of details that you think don't mean much or that seem silly, bizarre, or inconsequential. Imagine that the author—you in the robes of your dreaming consciousness—has a three-dimensional palette, plus the ability to improvise entire scenes in a fraction of a second using whatever props are handy, to create instant doors that open into new realities, sudden mirrors that show very different sides of you, and much, much more.

To your rational mind, dreaming isn't much more than a discombobulated madhouse operated by its inmates, but to your core of being, it's a multidimensional show mirroring all that you are in a dazzling array of fittingly costumed roles, inviting you to peer into the shadows.

You can begin working with your dreams by choosing one to reflect on. Here are some navigational guides to help you get started:

Recount your dream in the present tense, keeping your eyes closed. Do so as if you're speaking to a very interested, empathetic listener. This will help you more fully enter into the felt sense and subtext subtleties of your dream. Feel free to repeat or exaggerate certain lines, so long as doing so doesn't distract you from their flow.

Keep your intuitive radar on high. Listen to the narrative and emotional flow of your dream without getting caught up in analysis or interpretation. As much as possible, keep your attention undivided and your curiosity alive. Notice any associations that arise as you attune to your dream, but don't get sidetracked by them.

Notice personal details. Take note of your emotional state, body movements, and shifts in delivery as you recount your dream, registering these details at the same time that you're focusing on the content of the dream.

Remain aware of key highlights. If you lose track of parts of your dream—which often happens, especially with longer dreams—don't worry. Just stay present with what you can recall, tuning in to what stands out about the dream. When you start to work with your dream—and you don't have to start with the beginning—and bring more focus to the prevailing *feeling* of it, the parts you lost track of may return to you, in whole or in part. If they don't, stay with what you can remember.

Track the emotional quality of your dream from beginning to end. Listen very closely to every shift in the feeling tone of your dream as you speak it out loud, including when your voice goes flat, gets muted, or speeds up. Notice what these shifts stir in you, what elements of your personal history and the previous day's details surface.

Let go of having to find clear meaning. Sometimes you'll have no sense of what to make of a particular dream; this is quite natural. All you have to do is hold space for such dreams, putting no pressure on yourself to figure them out.

Reflect on all of the above for a bit, and then again recount your dream. Do so slowly, pausing after key points, taking note of further insights that may arise. You may find that later in the day—or even the next day or two—you receive more clarification about your dream.

Projection in Dreams

While we're in the waking state but not aware of our tendency to project, we just do it. For example, if we're conditioned to be nice and nonconfrontational, we can easily project our repressed anger onto others so that we get to see them as angry (whether they are or not) in contrast to us. While we're in the dreaming state, *we projectile project*, and the result is that our dreamscape is largely populated by beings, human and otherwise, that represent whatever in us we view as other than us. Furthermore, our dreams are filled with enough convincing realism and 3-D visuals to keep us, with few exceptions, taking the whole show as unquestioned reality.

To work with such projection, take a particular dream element—be it a person, an animal, or an object—and (1) speak as if you indeed *are* it, then (2) speak *to* it, and finally (3) speak *with* it, engaging in a back-and-forth dialogue between this element and you. (This process is described in detail in chapter 20, in the section titled "Further Steps in Working with Your Shadow.")

Here is a condensed example of working with projection in a dream:

> **Bob** I'm walking down a dark road, and I see a house with lights on ahead. I go inside and find a huge bear sleeping on the floor. It wakes up, looks at me, comes toward me. I'm really scared and can't move. It stands up, looking directly at me. This is all I remember.
>
> **Me** Close your eyes, breathe a bit deeper. . . . Now speak to the bear, as though you're right there in the house with it.
>
> **Bob** Please don't hurt me. Don't hurt me!
>
> **Me** Respond to what was just said, as if you're the bear speaking to the you in the dream.
>
> **Bob** (*as the bear*) I don't want to hurt you.
>
> **Me** Respond to this as yourself.
>
> **Bob** Why are you in this house? What are you doing here?
>
> **Me** Respond as if you're the bear.
>
> **Bob** (*as the bear*) I live here. I belong here!
>
> **Me** Hearing this, I feel . . .
>
> **Bob** (*tearing up*) Kind of relieved. (*long pause*)
>
> **Me** Now speak as though you are the house.
>
> **Bob** (*as the house*) I have room for both of you.

Bob had a domineering, *overbearing* father. As a boy he learned, for the sake of survival, to be very soft. The bear in his dream is his own power, slumbering until *he enters its space*. His dream was revealing that his power was in his shadow all this time, waiting for him to move toward it, to claim it, to take ownership of it.

Engaging in such work brings forth information and a felt know-ingness that might otherwise have remained all but inaccessible, closeted away somewhere in our shadow. We start to recognize that a particular dream element, however strange or alien, is in many cases none other than an aspect of us. Realizing this right to our core is a liberating experience, deepening our sense of wholeness; something that had been cast out of the circle of our being and into our shadow can now be recovered. This is a profoundly relevant reclamation project, a gathering in and reconnecting of our scattered parts so that they become *known* parts of the internal community which makes up our sense of self.

Additional Ways of Working with Dreams

Like shadow work, dream work requires us to turn toward whatever is arising, however challenging or nightmarish it is. It calls us to be willing to step into the dark, to look beyond appearances, to face what we ordinarily wouldn't face.

Because there are so many types of dreams, it's very helpful to have multiple ways of working with your dreams. Here are some.

Treat everything in your dream as if it's part of you. *Everything* doesn't just mean the other people in your dream, but also any animals, plants, things, objects. When working with a dream in this context, we take any part of the dream and, acting as if we're indeed that, *we speak as though we're it.* For example, there's a chair in our dream, so we start to spontaneously give it voice: "People like sitting on me" or "I'm tired of being sat on" or "Everyone takes me for granted." Whatever we say here, however negative, is revealing. The more fully we play out a part of our dream, the more fleshed out, exposed, and explicitly present it becomes.

Note: It's important to stay flexible here. If we believe that everything in our dream is never other than part of us, we'll then miss out on making good use of those dreams in which some things, some dream beings, are *not* parts of us. For example, if we're having trouble with our primary relationship, and our partner appears in our dreams, there's a good chance that their appearance may be as a representation of themselves, colored by our perception of them, rather than a representation of us. Some people may dream of being betrayed by their partner, and even though there's no obvious outward indication of such betrayal in waking life, their partner is, in fact, betraying them. Unable or unwilling to face this possibility in their everyday lives, these people have it surface in their dreaming, often with vivid impact.

In a psychotherapy session, Ed tells me that he has a recurring, terrifying nightmare of being pursued by a huge upright skunk with red eyes, from which he's unable to get away. As he describes this dream, he starts shaking, adding that he's had this dream since he was a boy. I ask him what was scariest for him as a child, and he says being sexually molested by his stepfather. What, I ask, did this man smell like? Ed says, "Really stinky"; his stepfather was a heavy drinker. And his eyes? "Red," says Ed, "especially when he came into my room."

Treat everything in your dream as though it's in relationship to every other part. Doing so can reveal connections that might otherwise go undetected. For example, in a dream we're driving a car with malfunctioning brakes. We begin working with this dream by imagining that we're the car. We talk to the driver, and then as the driver we respond to the car. As this back-and-forth dialogue continues, soon it becomes clear that we're proceeding in a certain area of our life without enough restraint (the details of the car and its surroundings may reveal which area of our life this is), putting ourselves at risk.

Treat everything in your dream as if it's worth considering. The details matter. Seemingly trivial things in a dream often are the tips of psychoemotional icebergs. What are you wearing in your dream? What's on the table? What do the front steps remind you of? What kind of wall is the mirror on? Be curious about every element of a dream, and if an element doesn't speak to you, speak *as though you are it*, at enough length to allow its interiority and emotional dimensions to surface.

Treat everything in your dream integrally. Approach your dream not just intellectually and psychologically but also emotionally, somatically, and spiritually, making room for the personal, interpersonal, and transpersonal to coexist in your exploration. This is a necessarily intuitive approach. Yes, use your capacity for metaphoric insight, but also tune in to the emotional texture and movement within the dream. Include your body. Acting out parts of a dream physically, assuming a posture that was in the dream—literally embodying gestures taken and untaken—all can further your understanding of your dream. When we're acting out a part of our dream that seems foreign to us, unusual openings and aha realizations may ensue.

Treat everything in your dream as though it's arising *within* you. Here you don't identify with anything in the dream—including the part you play in the dream—except for the *space* in the dream. Being this space, this immaterial container, is far from an abstract undertaking. It requires a nonconceptual shifting of perspective. The felt sense of this perspective is healthy detachment—detachment that doesn't dilute relationship. Though you may not explore a dream through this context very often, it is still worth having access to, especially when you're exploring the identity of the dreamer.

■

To really grasp the essence of a dream, we have to approach it with more than our mind, seeking revelation rather than just explanation. We must hear it without ears, see it without eyes, know it without thinking. We must cultivate as much intimacy as possible with both its detailing and its mystery. To work with our dreams is to get firsthand exposure to our shadow elements; we don't have to go digging for such elements. In the private shadow theatrics of our dreams, we meet more of what we are, along with the opportunity to find more understanding and more wholeness, including a wholeness beyond imagining.

PART THREE

PAIN

AND HOW TO
WORK WITH IT

26 BECOMING MORE INTIMATE WITH OUR PAIN

WE HAVE A SHADOW because there were things in us that we, for all sorts of reasons, were driven to flee, to dissociate or disconnect from, to keep in the dark. And we were driven to do so because we were in pain—in distress, in discomfort, in unresolvable hurt. To now deliberately turn toward this pain is a heroic step, furthering the warrior in us. Turning toward our pain and then exploring it, experiencing and knowing it from inside, is an essential part of working with our shadow, because our shadow is where our deepest pain is stored. *The more skillful we are in handling our pain, the better equipped we'll be for working with our shadow.*

We have the capacity to become intimate with our pain, step by conscious step. Along the way, we learn to enter our pain, differentiate it from suffering, investigate its various qualities, and eventually emerge from it. Genuine happiness doesn't require an absence of pain but rather that we face and consciously enter our pain. We may conceive of freedom as a pain-free domain, but real freedom is rooted not in being without pain but in how we handle it, how we relate to it, how intimate with it we choose to become. When we compassionately explore our pain, we sooner or later find ourselves settling into a sobering sense of okayness that doesn't necessarily disappear or disintegrate just because we're having a bad day.

Revisioning Our Pain

Pain is unpleasant sensation or feeling. Whoever we are, wherever we are, we inevitably experience pain. Yesterday's pain may still be occupying us, and tomorrow's pain too, together amplifying today's pain. We don't get what we want, and there's pain; we get what we don't want, and there's pain; and even when we get what we want, there's pain, if only because of how things change and how little in control of this we are.

Just as inevitably, we tend to store as much as possible of our pain in our shadow, finding strategies to numb, bypass, or otherwise get away from our pain. The more we try to flee the felt presence of pain—whether through denial, dissociation, or distraction—the more deeply it takes root in us, and not just in our shadow. So what are we to do?

The bare-bones answer begins with *turning toward our pain*, which means directly facing and feeling the raw reality of it. Then eventually we move closer to our pain, step by mindful step, gradually *entering it*, bringing our wholehearted awareness into its domain (as will be described in the next few chapters). And we start to recognize that *in order to emerge from our pain, we have to enter it*.

Often when we say that we're in pain, we're not really *in* our pain but rather only closer to it than we'd like. We're then in a sense still *outside* it, still cut off from its depths, still removed from its deeper interior.

But, we may ask, isn't the point to get rid of pain or to at least get away from it? After all, isn't pain already unpleasant enough? Why make it worse by moving closer to it, let alone entering it? These and similar questions are quite understandable, given our commonplace aversion to pain, be it physical, mental, emotional, or spiritual. The very notion of turning toward our pain and getting close enough to it to start knowing it well may initially seem counterintuitive, foolhardy, misguided, or masochistic.

There's no need to shame ourselves for turning away from our pain. It's enough to simply recognize such evasion for what it is. With this recognition we can bring in a compassionate exploration of the roots of such behavior, remembering and feeling our early-life efforts to get away from our pain, efforts that might have helped us survive very difficult circumstances but that now no longer serve us.

In turning toward our pain there's great freedom—a freedom that grounds us in our core of being. As we slowly but steadily undo our various ways of fleeing our pain, the energy we've invested in getting away from our pain—as opposed to simply *being with our pain*—is freed up, becoming available for us to use for truly life-giving purposes. Turning toward our pain doesn't increase our pain for very long, and actually decreases it relatively soon, mainly because we're no longer paining ourselves by putting so much energy into trying to get away from it. Also, turning toward our pain, thereby making more room for it, focuses and *expands* us, depressurizing and easing us, however slightly.

Being with our pain doesn't mean passively submitting to it or letting it run us but rather staying present with it, neither getting lost in it nor dissociating from it. It's easy to get overwhelmed by pain, spinning down into it as if being drawn down an energetic funnel toward a darkly contracted vortex. It's also easy to launch ourselves so far from it that we all but lose sight of it, settling into exaggerated detachment.

Remaining present with our pain may be far from easy, but with practice it's quite doable. And the more consistently present we can be with our pain, the less it pains us. It may still hurt, but we don't mind as much, for we're more able to hold it, to both contain it and express it under certain conditions (as when emotional release is clearly called for).

Despite pain's ubiquitous presence, day in and day out, our usual responses to it keep us from knowing it very well. It's not that there aren't times when it's entirely appropriate to get away from or take a break from pain, such as when it's debilitating or sharply out of control. But it's still entirely worthwhile learning how to simply *be with our pain*, staying present as possible in the midst of it.

There are many kinds of pain—physical, emotional, mental, psychological, existential—each of which has many qualities (such as density, texture, shape, and movement) that are all in flux. But the essence of each kind of pain is a compellingly felt sense of unpleasantness or discomfort, ranging from irritability to agony. That essence is what we encounter, hold, and become intimate with as we work with our pain, knowing it in both its detailing and core reality.

To turn toward our pain is to begin unhooking ourselves from our distractions from it. It's natural to seek distraction from our pain. Such evasion can take many forms—ranging from intellectual to pharmaceutical to erotic—any of which can easily dominate us, thereby disconnecting us from living a deeper life, if only by keeping us in the grip of our conditioning. The process of unhooking from these distractions is itself inevitably painful for a while, mostly because it hurts to wean ourselves from what we're habituated to doing. But soon it begins to feel okay, even when we're still hurting. The closer we get to our pain, the greater are the odds that we'll be able to skillfully relate *to* it rather than *from* it. When we thus relate *to* our pain, cultivating intimacy with it, *we start liberating ourselves from our pain and from the painful consequences of avoiding our pain.*

Pain can consume us, and our efforts to get away from pain can also consume us. When we turn away from our pain, seeking an escape from it, thereby avoiding knowing it and relating to it, *we entrap ourselves in our apparent solutions to our pain*, getting overly attached or addicted to whatever most pleasurably or reliably removes us from it. This, however, just generates more pain and drains our energy reserves without at all resolving the original pain. The good news here is that the inherent dissatisfaction of such pain-avoiding strategies—especially when they manifest as addictiveness—sooner or later points us, however roughly, in more life-giving directions.

As much as we may wish pain wasn't there, it abides, offering us the same basic opportunity: to cease avoiding it so that we might use it for life-giving purposes, allowing it to further open our eyes and root us in truer ground. This doesn't mean that pain is some sort of wonderful gift but rather that pain's openly felt presence has the capacity to funnel our attention into single-pointed focus, gathering us into a lucid wholeness, however compressed, rather than fragmenting us.

Go to the heart of your pain and you won't find more pain but rather a freedom that doesn't require the absence of pain.

Pain Versus Suffering

In everyday speech, *pain* and *suffering* are used interchangeably. However, pain and suffering differ considerably from each other. Yes, to suffer is to be in pain, but to be in pain isn't necessarily to suffer.

Pain is fundamentally just unpleasant—sometimes extremely unpleasant—sensation or feeling. Suffering, on the other hand, is something that we're *doing* with our pain. Compare:

> **Pain**   My husband just left me, and I'm hurting terribly. My heart is broken.
>
> **Suffering**   My husband just left me, and I'm hurting terribly. My life is over. I'll never find love again. My mother's right—I should never have been born.

When we can't sufficiently distract ourselves from our pain, we often turn it into suffering, in two overlapping ways:

Resisting our pain. This is when we adopt an adversarial relationship to our pain. What's in our shadow here is the raw reality of our pain *and* our acceptance of it.

Dramatizing our pain. This is when we make an unpleasantly gripping tale out of our pain, centered by our hurt "I." What's in our shadow here is our investment in this drama.

As gripping as suffering can be—and at times it can be overwhelming—it's usually optional, in much the same sense that reactivity is optional. When we're suffering, we're not only resisting the bare reality of our pain but we're also busy *identifying* with it, *overpersonalizing* it, thereby entrapping ourselves not only in our pain but also in our dramatization of it.

Where pain is consciously felt hurt, suffering is the myopic *dramatization* of that hurt, casting us in the role of the hurt one and binding us there. We're *occupied by* our hurt role to such an extent that we've little or no motivation to see through or stand apart from it. Thus we keep ourselves from the raw reality of our pain and the opportunity to become intimate with it.

The degree to which we allow our pain to turn into suffering is the degree to which we obstruct our own healing and well-being. When we're busy suffering, we're *avoiding* simply being present with the nonconceptual rawness of our pain. The very energy we're putting into this aversion, this desperation to be elsewhere, is energy that's not available for more life-giving purposes. Suffering may *seem* to keep us near our pain—after all, there's no doubt that we're hurting—but in fact suffering *separates* us from our pain. It prevents us from getting as close to our pain as we need to be, if we're to live a more liberated life.

To work effectively with our suffering, we need both to stand apart from its script, so as to more clearly bring it into focus, and to cease distancing ourselves from our pain. As we step back from the dramatics of our suffering, we not only start seeing through our role as the sufferer but also start seeing our investment in that role. We might still be hooked, but we're not *as* hooked, especially as we become more attentive to the naked reality of our pain.

When we turn on the lights, the dramatics of suffering become transparent. Then the uncensored reality of our pain gets our full attention, allowing us to explore our pain with care, clarity, and precision. We start to know it from the inside, noticing its fluxing weave and interplay of qualities. Instead of just having a blanket sense of our pain, we sense it in living detail. *We cease resisting it.*

It's in the conscious and compassionate—and unresisting—entry into our pain that we begin to find some real freedom from our suffering. Our hurt may remain, but the way that we relate to it will have changed. Instead of fighting it we're holding it.

Suffering is a refusal to develop any intimacy with our pain. When we're busy suffering, we're without healthy detachment; we're removed from the direct reality of our pain but not in a way that permits us to focus more clearly on what's actually occurring. Pain doesn't necessarily obstruct happiness, but suffering does. In fact, suffering only incarcerates our pain, keeping it overly contained, too tightly confined.

But as we turn away from the screens upon which our suffering projects its stories, we begin to awaken. Gradually our increasingly embodied awareness upstages our suffering, dissolving more and more of its grip on us, taking us to the heart, the core, the epicenter, of our pain. And there, in that place of hurt, we meet not more hurt but more us—more healing, more peace, more welcome. We start freeing ourselves from our suffering by bringing the raw reality of our pain completely out of our shadow. In so doing, we increase the odds that our pain will serve rather than obstruct us.

Turning toward our pain reduces our suffering. Entering our pain further reduces our suffering. Moving through our pain ends or at least radically reduces our suffering, even if our pain remains. The more intimate we are with our pain, the less we suffer.

27 TURNING TOWARD OUR PAIN

TURNING TOWARD OUR PAIN *means facing and unresistingly feeling its raw reality.* Along with taking an eyes-open look at the actual pain we're in, we need to consider how this pain is connected to or expressive of the wounding we experienced in our early years. If we're not aware of how this past hurt may be affecting us today and of how many of our current behaviors are attempts to avoid feeling such hurt, then we're tethered to our past, unable to be fully present and whole *now*.

Turning toward our pain means bringing into our heart what we have rejected in ourselves, what we've ostracized, disowned, neglected, bypassed, shunned, excommunicated, or otherwise deemed as unworthy—namely, all that we've kept in our shadow. Common examples include our shame, rage, envy, and greed. Opening ourselves to such qualities doesn't, however, mean that we then allow them to run the show, to act out, to run wild, any more than we would allow a child—including our own reclaimed child side—to drive our car down a freeway. We need to proceed here with great care, sidestepping the minefields of overtolerance and let's-accept-it-all naiveté, keeping our eyes simultaneously open and discerning.

When something has been caged for a long while, kept for prolonged periods from much of what it needs, it probably won't behave very well when released. Knowing this, we won't expect our pain to tamely resonate with our expectations when we're no longer protecting or distracting ourselves from it.

Initially it's enough to simply name our pain—saying, for example, that we're hurting, anxious, or lonely—and remain turned toward it, taking our time to get to know it.

Before reaching for your favorite fix, simply ask yourself what you're actually feeling besides your urge to thus reach. *Then turn toward that feeling,* giving it your undivided attention and staying with it, allowing yourself to fully feel it—as though it's a distraught child you love and are holding. By doing so, you increase the likelihood that you won't distract yourself from your pain, including through any addictive behavior.

Deepening Our Stand

In acknowledging our pain, we may still be turned away from it. However, when we turn toward our pain, turning until we're facing it directly, we're in a position to prepare ourselves to step forward. And this begins with *deepening our stand.*

Deepen it we must, or we will be uprooted too easily. As we strengthen and stabilize our stand, getting more used to facing our pain, we may notice that our longing to be truly free is, however slightly, getting stronger than our longing to distract ourselves from our pain.

We're now facing the dragon of pain, perhaps feeling its heat and meaty threat as we open ourselves to its presence, but not so much as to overwhelm ourselves. We hold our position in a manner that settles and further anchors us. We may feel like distracting ourselves, but we have too much at stake—and now really know that we have too much at stake—to postpone, obstruct, or otherwise turn away from our pain. So we stay put, but not rigidly. And if we find it too difficult to stand where we are, we step back a bit and anchor ourselves there.

Once you've turned toward your pain and have found a position where you know you can take a stand with adequate solidity, root yourself there. Here's a practice to reinforce this:

PRACTICE

Stand tall and breathe deeply. As you exhale, envision the stand you're taking slowly streaming down through your torso into your legs and feet, and then through the soles of your feet into the earth.

And as you inhale, envision your stand rising up through you, flowing up through your feet, legs, and torso, lengthening your spine and lifting your sternum, reaching your head, which balances effortlessly but solidly atop your neck. Your gaze is both focused and soft. Repeat this energy-circulating visualization for at least ten breaths.

Even if you're shaking inside, perhaps sweating at the thought of more fully encountering the pain you're facing, maintain your full height, filling out your body with presence as best you can, so that you begin to get at least some sense of embodying your true size. No matter how slight this shift is, stay with it, breathing strength into your intention to stand your ground. But do not move forward yet.

Beware of any ambition that would have you move forward prematurely. Beware of any investment in playing the hero, the impeccable warrior, male or female. What matters is that you take a stand and do all you can not to wander away from it. You may sway in the wind, you may wish you were elsewhere, you may tremble, but don't let this turn you away from your pain.

As you ground yourself, keep some awareness of the back of you, doing so with as little strain as possible. "See" with the back of your head, your shoulder blades, your sacrum, the back of your heart, the small of your back, sensing what's behind you while not losing sight of what's before you.

Stay with this practice for at least five minutes.

Give yourself enough time to acclimatize to deepening your stand. Directly facing your pain, which includes facing your aversion to it, may be a very new experience for you. If your pain seems grotesque or repellent, it may be because you've treated it as such, keeping it from compassionate contact so long that it has taken up residence in distorted forms.

As you stand your ground, cultivate a second-person relationship with your pain, which means relating *to* it. Before, you probably had a first-person approach to your pain—that is, *identifying* with it—as well as a third-person approach to it, meaning keeping your pain as an unpleasant or undesirable "it" somewhere in the distance (just as you may have considered your body to be an "it" somewhere *below* your "headquarters"). So now instead of relating *from* your pain or treating it as an "it" to keep as far away as possible, you relate *to* it. You listen to it. You observe it without disengaging from it. You let yourself sense more than its surface features. You start cultivating some intimacy with it, no matter how alien it might seem. And you keep whatever distance you need to maintain your stand, relocating if you have to, without turning away to any significant degree.

If cultivating a relationship with your pain sounds like something you think you can't do, think again: to turn toward your pain doesn't necessarily mean that you remain thus positioned all the time. As long as you keep turning toward your pain, and practice staying there, rooted as best you can, it won't really matter that you weren't able to always stay with it for very long. Acclimatization takes a while.

So take enough time for the necessary adaptation. Treat the process more like a long hike over rough terrain rather than sprint training. Facing your pain decreases its grasp on you and builds your courage. Practice with little pains, pains that seem too small to fuss over, getting as familiar as possible with the art of bringing your full attention to your pain.

Turning toward our pain is a big step toward real personal freedom. In turning toward our pain, we're also turning toward others' pain (in both personal and collective contexts). One result of this is that our compassion for others not only deepens but also widens, eventually excluding none, no matter how different from us they are. So turn as slowly as you need to, but do turn. You're worth it. So are we.

28 NAMING AND ENTERING OUR PAIN

NAMING OUR PAIN helps reinforce our capacity to face it. Entering our pain is the next step after turning toward our pain and deepening our stand with it.

Naming Our Pain

In naming our pain—verbally acknowledging its presence—we begin, however slightly, to relate to it. We're taking just enough space from our pain to keep it in clear view. If we stand too far apart from our pain, we lose touch with it, and if we get too close to it, we lose ourselves in it.

After such naming—which could, as a label-giving exercise only, overseparate us from our pain—our next step is to more directly face our pain, to move a bit *closer* to it. Following is a four-step practice for naming and moving closer to your pain, including things to keep in mind as you proceed.

PRACTICE

1. Initially just say to yourself, under your breath, "Pain," "Pain is here," or "I'm in pain." Doing this may sound very simple, but it's not so easy to do *only* this. You may be tempted to quickly shift from naming it to pumping energy and attention into its storyline. By getting absorbed in *that*, you unwittingly turn your pain into suffering.

Not that the storyline doesn't matter, but in the beginning, when we've just named our pain, it's important to stay for a significant amount of time with the raw feeling of our pain. Thinking about the circumstances of our pain at this point isn't very helpful, for in so doing we mostly only distract ourselves from the basic reality of what's occurring.

What's important here is to let the bare presence of your pain register, letting yourself openly feel it. *Don't let your desire to avoid your pain separate you from it.*

2. Once you've named your pain, remain as present with it as you can, giving it your undivided attention. Instead of thinking about your pain, keep aware *of* it.

There's no anti-intellectual bias in this, just some foundational practicality. If we name our pain and then jump into thinking, rethinking, and then thinking some more about it, we'll very soon be suffering, wrapped up in the overdramatization of hurt, with us in the starring role.

3. Let the felt acknowledgment of your pain, initiated through your naming of it, resonate through you as much as possible. Give it time to settle in you. If you start to lose touch with this process, name your pain again. Don't try to analyze, interpret, or explain it. You can do so later, but for now it's enough to simply be with it as it is.

In short, stick to the data. Distinguish between stating data—bare facts—and stating perceptions. Statements such as "He's not there for me" or "I feel as if no one cares about me" are open to debate. But saying "I feel sad" or "My shoulders are hurting" isn't debatable information.

If I'm angry and I tell you that I'm angry, I'm simply sharing data. If I'm angry and I tell you that you're making me feel like dropping our whole relationship, I'm not sharing data but rather perception, opinion, a particular view. So after you've named your pain, stick to the data if you choose to say more about what's going on for you.

4. As you settle into the straightforward acknowledgment of your pain—which you've named as "pain"—you can then take the naming a step further by getting as *specific* as you can about what kind of pain it is.

You can describe your pain not only according to its qualities—shape, intensity, texture, movement, color, density—but also, if possible, its position in the pantheon of pain categories: physical pain, frustration, hurt, shame, anger, numbness, worry, anxiety, depression, and so on.

Also, you can describe where in your body you sense your pain—and what you're doing with it. Again, don't get lost in subjective reporting ("I don't feel seen" or "I feel let down"). Instead, make it simple and factual, stating what's nondebatable ("I feel disgust," "My belly is tight," or "I'm irritated").

■

Sense your pain, bring it into focus, and name its presenting qualities, but if it remains amorphous or otherwise descriptively elusive, just saying "pain" or "I'm hurting" is enough. Then note as best you can how it's manifesting physically, mentally, emotionally.

Naming and describing your pain marks the beginning of cultivating intimacy with it. It may still feel horrible, but at least you're not so identified with it, not so lost in it. Darkness may still be enwrapping and contracting you, but there's some light, some flickering of recognition. Pay closer attention and that flickering will sooner or later flame more brightly.

In the process of naming your pain, your primary intention is embodied focusing and unguarded openness. You feel your pain and acknowledge its presence but you haven't yet moved significantly closer to it. You're gathering data, as in a preliminary field survey, and you're just beginning to make room in yourself for what you have to do, without escaping into abstraction.

The following can help us in naming our pain:

- Knowing ourselves, our conditioning, and what occupies our shadow.

- Developing more emotional literacy—recognizing what we're feeling as we feel it.

- Being with others who won't let us off the hook when we're mishandling our pain.

- Practicing naming whatever is arising in us—and not just the unpleasant or difficult stuff.

- Recognizing how distracting ourselves from our pain prevents us from being fully alive.

- Choosing to no longer numb ourselves, no matter how much that may hurt.

When we look back and recognize how not naming our pain has hurt us—for example, by unnecessarily prolonging our pain and turning it into suffering—we'll be more open to naming it.

What are you feeling right now? Whatever it is, name it. Keep it simple. Then turn toward it with your undivided attention and curiosity.

Entering Our Pain

Once you've turned toward your pain and you're not swayed from continuing to do so, you've begun to enter your pain. You may be only ankle-deep in the shallow end of the pool, but you're nonetheless in it. You're now moving into shadow material.

What you've done to arrive here has prepared you to go further. If you simply had been deposited here, like a tourist lowered from a helicopter onto Everest's summit, you would likely not fare very well, given your lack of preparation and seasoning.

What follows is a sequence of steps for skillfully entering your pain:

1. Notice if you're resisting your pain in any way—including by letting it morph into suffering. Also notice any investment you might have in so doing. Keep disengaging from—ceasing to identify with—your suffering "I."

2. As you take your embodied awareness into your pain and your expression of it, notice that however much the unpleasantness of your sensations may persist, you simultaneously feel a touch more spacious. Your pain, however intense or turbulent, is more vivid and clearly defined, trimmed of any buffering, any of suffering's dark furnishing and cushioning.

3. Move close enough to your pain that there's negligible distance between it and you—just enough to keep it in focus. Allow your attention to reach beneath the presenting surface of your pain. Breathe more deeply. Make each step, each extending of attention, as conscious as possible.

4. As you move into your pain, inching into its contracted and often poorly lit geography, you may find that you're not moving in a straight line. So be it. The ground might be far from level, shaky with emotional intensity. So be it.

5. Bring as much attention as possible to your pain's qualities—its texture, movements, density, temperature, shaping, intensity, and so on—without getting lost in them. Notice their shifts. (For more on these qualities, see chapter 29.) To enter your pain is to unguardedly feel into and observe it and its various qualities. Sense your way in, with your attention alert and spacious, noticing how things are changing as you deepen your investigation. As you progress, you'll recognize firsthand that your pain isn't as simple as it might seem; instead, it's a complex phenomenon, with

physical, emotional, mental, and social dimensions, all in fluxing interplay with each other.

6. When you're working with emotional hurt, there's a difference between saying "I'm feeling sad" and "I feel that no one cares about me." Stick to the first sort of description, which is factual, and avoid the second, which is perceptual, interpretive, constructed, open to debate. Keeping to the first approach allows you to stay focused on your pain, whereas getting into the second approach easily generates and reinforces suffering.

7. Continue scanning your pain and its qualities. Instead of being removed from your pain, stranding yourself in a sterilized objectivity, you're starting to become intimate with your pain, employing a *radical subjectivity* in your approach to it. You're very close to it, immersed in it, openly feeling and perhaps expressing it, but you're also keeping just enough distance to be able to keep a clear eye on it.

You're now encountering your pain not from behind glass or from a tour bus but directly, like a traveler immersed in a foreign yet oddly familiar culture, venturing into a fresh adventure armed only with curiosity and the spirit of open-eyed investigation.

The further you consciously venture into your pain, the less you suffer, so long as you proceed at a pace that allows you to stay grounded and present. You may still hurt, you may still shake with anger or fear, you may still squirm with shame, but you're not making a binding story out of it. As your pain is given more space, more breathing room, it usually becomes less gripping, less commanding, less problematic, even when it still really hurts.

After a while, we'll sense our pain shifting into a vivid presence that both sharpens our focus and deepens us, regardless of its discomfort. It's as if we've just reached a wild river's headwaters; there's still plenty of churning and turbulence, but in its deep currents we can feel an immense spaciousness. This is the heartland of our pain, the epi-center out of which our experience of our pain flows forth. Reaching this place is a great turning point; we've gone in as far as we can, and now we're in sight of emerging on the other side of pain, carrying with us the gifts and lessons of having entered it so deeply.

Here there arises a primal sense of okayness that coexists with our discomfort. We still may hurt, but we don't mind all that much; we've ceased letting our pain go to mind. We're neither trying to get rid of it nor to get away from it. Instead, we're simply with it, allowing its contractedness to soften, giving it room to mutate.

We're inside the dragon now, feeling its pulse, its dark density, its ancient appetite. And we're refusing to be its latest meal. Instead of it having its way with us, eating or eating at us, we're in a sense eating *it*—taking it in, digesting it, emerging through it. We're not trapped by its scaly bulk and threatening nature. We don't have to slay the dragon, for as we enter its interior, passing behind its eyes and fiery front, we make its energies ours, bringing ourselves more and more alive. Then the fire of the dragon is not only heat to us but also light. This is the core of shadow work. We're now mining our pain.

This is the experiential alchemy of grounded transformation, planting us in the bedrock of being, while our adversarial relationship with our pain fades.

29 EXPLORING THE QUALITIES OF PAIN

EXPLORING THE QUALITIES of our pain helps us deepen our intimacy with our pain—and the more intimate we're able to be with our pain, the less we suffer. The detail I go into in this chapter is meant to help deepen and refine your capacity to have an up-close, multidimensional sense of your pain.

Pain's Directionality

Some pain seems to squat in us like a solid mass, dense and packed with inertia. But other pain—most pain, in fact—possesses a felt sense of movement, a directionality. Such movement may sometimes not seem to be going in any particular direction. For example, it may be prickly with erratic back-and-forth movements, or it may be more rounded or blunted, pulsing with some regularity but with no discernible direction. Plenty of pain, however, has a clearer directionality, with its energies mostly moving inwardly, outwardly, or upwardly.

Pain that's moving inwardly. Usually this kind of pain has a strong degree of contractedness, as if its forces are being drawn toward a core of sorts, narrowing and intensifying on the way. The sensations are of being crushed, compressed, sucked into a vortex, and other *centripetal* forms of contraction. Infiltrating and amplifying—and often generating—these sensations is the emotional quality of our pain, generally rooted in fear, shame, or sadness. We're not so much down and out as *down and in*. Quite often there may be a sensation of being flattened or pressed down—hence, *de-pression*.

Pain that's moving outwardly. This sort of pain is more expansive than inward-bound pain, but it still hurts. Why? Because its expansiveness actually contains plenty of contraction. A fist moving outwardly is still a fist, a hardened ball of tightly gripped force. An example of outwardly moving pain is that associated with expressed anger. We may give our anger heated expression, expanding our energy field considerably, feeling a sense of upper-body inflation, but we're still contracted; there's a knotted tension in our hands, jaw, eyes, belly.

The directionality of sadness, though often inward—as in depression—can also be outward. This is most obvious in unrestrained grief, in which there's a powerful upswelling and outpouring of deeply felt hurt and loss, surging forth like an undammed river or storm.

Pain that's moving upwardly. Pain's directionality sometimes may seem to be *upwardly* aimed, as when in anger we feel as though we're "going through the roof" or "about to blow our lid." The pain here feels pressurized, tightly contained, especially at the top end of the container—our throat, jaw, head.

Another sort of upwardly moving pain is that of emotional hurt getting stuck in our high chest and throat, its expression suppressed. There may be something important to say, but our throat and jaw are clamped or constricted enough to block it.

Pain that's on the move. Pain can also move in other directions. It may, for example, find diagonal pathways. When I had a near-fatal heart attack in 2016, my pain at its peak pulsed with killing intensity from deep within the center of the lower left side of my chest to the rear of my outer left shoulder and down the inside of my left upper arm.

There's also zigzag pain: stabbing headaches and migraines, inner-ear hurt, going back and forth between painful alternatives, agonizing dilemmas.

If our pain is on the move, is it doing so inwardly, outwardly, upwardly, or in some other way? Notice where in your body this is most evident. Notice how strong or compelling such movement is. How far into your body does it seem to go, and where in your body is it the most intense? Are you being inwardly pushed, pulled, or both? And if so, is there any rhythm to it?

We can be swept or pulled along by our pain's directionality, as if we're unable to do anything other than go wherever it takes us. Or we can become aware of our pain's directionality so that even though it continues, *we become the space in which it's happening while simultaneously letting ourselves directly and openly feel it.*

Pain's Texture

To detect pain's texture—or tactile feel and weave—we have to pay very close, finely focused attention to it, as if we're slowly running our mind's hand over and over it. At first, we'll probably only have a very broad, rather vague sense of its texture, classifying our pain according to its degree of sharpness or roughness. Later on, though, we'll access a more precise and nuanced way of feeling into and describing its texture. The kinds of questions to ask, and keep asking, are:

- How sharp is my pain?

- Is its sharpness spear-like or bristly?

- Is it finely stabbing or more bluntly edged?

- How soft is my pain?

- How thick is its softness, how heavy, and how is it surfaced?

- Does it feel at all rubbery or silky, or sandpapery, mushy, crinkly, or jagged?

- How porous is my pain?

- If I had to wear it, how would it feel against my skin?

- When I soften the areas around my pain, what happens to its texture?

- Has the texture of my pain changed at all in the last minute or two? And if so, how?

MAKING OUR DESCRIPTION OF OUR PAIN LESS ABSTRACT

Think of how much is being said when you share touch with an intimate. Plenty of what's communicated eludes translation. We can say that the touch feels good, or nice, or that we love the one we're doing this with. But to get more precise, we have to at some point get more poetic and evocative, because the prosaic—in which language marches rather than dances—just doesn't do justice to what's happening. The same with pain.

Saying that pain hurts or doesn't feel good is a starter, but using these simple terms is much like trying to make intimate contact with another through touch while wearing thick, stiff gloves. We need to take the gloves off and let ourselves really feel what's there—literally get more in touch with it—while giving our language as much poetic license as we need. We might then, for example, say that our pain feels like a wriggling scaly fist, or an itchy blanket wrapped around an oblong bonfire, or a darkly undulating quicksand.

The less abstract our descriptions of our pain are, the closer we get to it.

If you're getting "hot under the collar," you may well be "losing your cool," getting close to "blowing your lid." Such language doesn't just mean that we're angry. It also conveys, with a streetwise poetics, something about the experiential nature of our upset. Telling you that I'm "hot under the collar" gives you more information than would just informing you that I'm angry. I'm more than "simmering" but not yet at the stage of "boiling." I'm not about "to blow a gasket," but I'm definitely more than just mildly irritated.

Touch your pain the way that you would touch something delicate in a room devoid of light—carefully, sensitively, consciously, letting as many sensations as possible register, feeling your way in, along, and through. Stay in touch with the texture of your pain, however uncomfortable it may be. Let what you're touching touch you, so that whatever contact is being made reaches your depths.

Pain's Temperature

The investigation of pain's temperature may seem to be just a matter of pointing to a particular place on a flat, sliding scale: at one end we have very cold and at the other end very hot. Anger is closer to the hot end (with the exception of icily held anger), and depressive sadness closer to the cold end. Other kinds of pain may wander all over the scale—anxiety, for example, can sweatily ricochet between heated agitation and churned-up chill.

The sense of heatedness or coolness may be steady or may fluctuate. Are its waves infrequent or do they arrive more closely together? Does the heat warm or burn, soothe or scare? Does the cold refresh or chill? Is the cold dry or damp?

Sensing not just the general temperature of our pain but also the fine shifts and turns in temperature brings us closer to our pain. We might think that an increase in pressure would mean an increase in temperature, but this isn't necessarily so. A pressing outward, as is commonly felt in anger, generally brings up the temperature (hence all the fire metaphors for anger), but a pressing inward is more likely to chill us, as exemplified by depression or claustrophobia.

It's interesting to consider shame here, for it initially brings a certain heatedness—often reddening our face—even though it's contracting us inwardly. Shame exposes us—like we've been caught red-handed—and we quickly shrink, as if to minimize our exposure, our painful nakedness, our sheer mortification. As our shame continues, the initial rush of facial warmth, a humid heatedness, subsides and we continue to shrink and deflate, *cooling down*, unless we convert our shame into aggression. Shame's heat is muggy and invasive, arriving more as a suffocating blanket than a bolt.

Fear and anger represent the greatest emotional polarity when it comes to pain's temperature. Anxiety and worry may rev us up, but they leave us far from warm. Dread and terror are much chillier; we may sweat, but it's damp and cold.

Anger is plentifully supplied with heat and fire metaphors. We may be "doing a slow burn" or "have smoke coming out of our ears." We may be about to "erupt." The pressure implied in these phrases suggests an increase in temperature. Anger's liquid-like yet fiery bodily coursings—which we might call a full-blooded electricity—provide an intense immediacy of heatedness. Abruptly, we're "charged up," "bursting with rage," or "flooded with fury." Once I'm "plugged in," I can "blast" you, or perhaps make some "inflammatory" remarks. I may even get so "amped up" or "fired up" that I "go ballistic!" That's how hot anger can get.

Bring a finely focused attention to your pain's temperature, almost as if you have heat sensors mounted on the scanner of your attention. Do more, if you can, than simply using "hot" and "cold" labels—note the kind of heat, the kind of cold. Let your description indicate how you're actually experiencing your pain's temperature.

Pain's Color

Pain's color is a matter not of collectively agreed-upon visual certainty but rather personal internal sensing in which we feel the fit of a particular color or colors with a particular state. Though some colors are almost universally associated with certain states—such as red and black with anger, or gray with depression—pain's colors and color palette are, in general, uniquely cast for each individual.

We may not have any sense of color in mind for our pain when we're in it, but if we pay closer attention to our pain and ask ourselves what color or colors it seems to have, usually some sort of color or sense of coloration will emerge. We may not visually register the purple, dull red, or yellowishness, but we *feel* these colors and "see" them through such feeling. They fit. And as we watch closely, we may see them mutating, especially as we more fully enter our pain.

When we're angry, we may "see red" or sense ourselves in "a black rage." If we go far enough, we may suffer a blackout or red-out. And why red? Because of the fieriness of our anger, the heat and pressure of it, the flushed imperatives of it. Few would describe their anger as pale red or pink; it's usually a bright or dark red.

We can literally turn red not only with anger but also with shame. However, redness is usually not as strongly associated with shame, because shame moves not upward and outward like anger, but downward and inward. Our redness fades; it gets muddied by this interior, sinking pull so that much of what we sense is an amorphous, shady blending or overlapping of relatively indistinct colors. And the fact that shame tends to be converted quite quickly into other states—withdrawal, avoidance, aggression, mental fogginess—brings in a different color palette.

If we have preconceived notions linking color with emotion—such as dark green with jealousy—it's best to put them aside as we examine the colors of our pain. As we turn toward our pain, we may not sense any particular color, but as we enter our pain, we usually will begin sensing various colors, including black. We can then attune to the intensity of the color, the shading of it, the thickness or streakiness of it, along with the way it varies with other qualities such as directionality and texture.

Notice if the colors that you sense or intuit have movement in them. Do they arrive in flashes, or like a tide rolling in, or are they just slapped on? Are they in layers? Do they shift as you bring attention to them? When your pain intensifies, does its coloring change, and if so, how?

Sometimes your pain may seem to become more illuminated, lit up, even incandescent. Sometimes it may emanate the softest of light, in varying shades of white or pale yellow. Other times it may seem to be washed free of any color or just be plain black.

Whatever the coloring, keep an eye on it, observing it with undivided, spacious attentiveness.

Pain's Density and Intensity

By *pain's density*, I mean the felt sense of the weightiness, the thickness, the specific gravity or mass-increasing contractedness of our pain. By *pain's intensity* I mean the degree of our pain's felt forcefulness, ranging from minimally irritating to unbearable.

The greater our pain's density, the greater its intensity: Is this true? Not necessarily. Depression is dense but usually not as intense as, say, panic or fury. Density may be alive with tremendously vibrant energy, or it may simply be inertia doing time beneath leaden covers.

Sometimes when we have gotten inside our pain, it may seem to thicken and/or intensify. It helps to know that an increase in the density of neural firing—usually sensed as an increase in adrenaline—can generate fear, excitement, anger, passion. The stimulation for this increase doesn't have to be negative; when it's positive, we may still be pushed over a physiological threshold into emotional pain. Too much of a good thing can, in other words, easily backfire, turning our positive excitation into a less-than-pleasant agitation, a distressing intensity.

Take your attention into your pain's intensity, noting its degree of difficulty and how you're relating to that. Also notice the quality of its presence: Is it steady, rhythmic, pushing, pulling, arriving in waves or bolts? Does it seem wide or narrow, steep or shallow? How does it affect your breathing, your posture, your solar plexus, your eyes, your throat, your tongue? How close to unbearable is it?

Perhaps at the same time, observe your pain's density, slowly but surely penetrating it, feeling your way into its thickness and weightiness. Does it seem as if you have to squeeze your awareness into it? Does it seem to weigh on you, and if so, is it pushing down on you or pulling you from below? If your pain's density is a forest, how far apart are the trees? How much light are they letting in? How solid are their trunks, how deep their roots, how entangled their branches?

As you go into your pain's density, see if you can create more space within it, as if you're elbowing out more room for yourself. Sometimes the simple act of taking your attention into such density will make it more porous, less heavy. Lightening the density of our pain not only by consciously entering it but also by accessing compassion for ourselves *and* others in similar positions can make our pain's intensity more manageable.

In working with our pain's intensity, it's very helpful to focus on the areas immediately surrounding our pain. Doing what we can to *soften* and ease these areas gives the intensity a bigger place in which to spread out, thereby decreasing its degree of contraction. Our pain's intensity may still be a fist, but it's now less firmly clenched, like a stone statue that, though holding its shape, registers a cracking or unwinding from within, an upcoming de-densification, a shift from rock to sand.

Pain's Shape

Pain has a shape? Sometimes, yes, but not necessarily in any measurable form. It often initially registers as a subtle construct, coming into focus as we become aware of its topography. To sense and stay current with our pain's shape and shaping, we have to scan it three-dimensionally, touring its contours as if we're in a low-flying plane equipped with both depth vision and peripheral vision.

Discerning our pain's shape is a bit like taking note of the shape and shaping of a wave, even as it breaks and is gone; we may recall it briefly, holding a fleetingly crystallized image or two of it, but we're already scanning the next wave.

Consider pain that takes shape as something roughly approximating a sphere. Sense its diameter, location, solidity, symmetry. Check it out from all sides, without expecting it to hold still as you do so. Does it show up as roundness wherever you scan it? Inspect it for dents, dimples, cracks, elliptical breakaways. Also try scanning it from the inside. Is it hollow, solid, semisolid? How dense is it? Is it expanding, contracting, or holding steady?

Does your pain have corners? If so, how sharp or precise are they? Does your pain seem to have extensions, roots, fjords, canyons, tendrils? Does your pain's shape flow? And if so, how? Is its flow silky, amoeboid, disclike, prickly, staccato, twirling, jagged?

Attuning ourselves to our pain's shape and shaping allows us to track it more closely. To remain thus attuned requires that we stay present with our pain, since its spatial reality usually doesn't keep static for very long.

Bring your attention toward and into your pain. Sense where it is in your body. Once you are steadily present with your pain, ask yourself what its shape is. Don't worry about getting it verbally right; trust your intuition. Three-dimensionally frame your pain with awareness, being careful to keep this framing limited to a size that keeps it from touching or pressing in on your pain. Then deepen your scanning of your pain's shape, as if examining a deep-sea marvel that has shown up in your imaginal netting. Whatever is happening, sense its shape and shaping. Don't try to pin it down or freeze it; simply encounter it. If it's a lump, fine; if it's a winged alien, fine; if it's nothing in particular, fine.

See your pain's shaping; touch it, ski and surf and trek it, keeping an eye on its totality even as you zoom in on various details. The more curious you are, the better. Formulate and answer questions about the shape of your pain, along the lines of:

- Does it come all the way up to your head?

- How far down does it go in your body?

- Is the back of it shaped like the front?

- Are its contours smooth? Edgy? Undulating? Squishy?

- Is your pain shaped like a club, a funnel, an hourglass, a deflated ball, a brick?

- Has the shape of your pain changed at all in the last minute or so? And if so, how?

Whatever shape our pain may be in, we can deeply benefit from keeping a close eye on it. *Staying informed about the form of our pain makes room for our pain to transform*, to shift from a problematic something into an energetic, ever-fluxing presence that helps deepen our awareness.

30 EMERGING FROM OUR PAIN

THE MORE THAT WE move through the sequence of turning toward, naming, entering, and being with our pain, the easier it tends to get, until it's not so much a sequence as an evolving responsiveness in which the steps of working with our pain organically coexist and overlap. We don't reach a point where we're done with pain, but we become increasingly skillful in making wise use of it.

As we cease viewing our pain as nothing more than a problem, we cut through our resentment over having it. Knowing that *everything*, including pain, can serve our healing and awakening then becomes less of an idea and more of a living reality.

Each time we're in pain and choose to face and enter it, we reduce our suffering. Each time we find our way to the core of our pain, we're reawakened, released, reestablished in our heartland, no matter how tired, ill, or emotionally rocked we may be. When we don't thus journey, the reminders of not doing so—our closures of heart, energetic tightness, existential isolation—usually don't take all that long to register.

As we proceed, being okay with not being okay becomes commonplace. Pain then is far less likely to submerge us so easily. Again and again we emerge, feeling the satisfaction of having made good use of a challenging circumstance. We don't reach this emergence through engaging in any sort of bypassing—spiritual, intellectual, or otherwise—but through entering into and becoming intimate with our pain. When we say that we're in pain, we need to make sure that we're indeed *in* it rather than outside it or removed from it.

To emerge from our pain, we have to enter it. To do otherwise is to suffer. And emerging from our pain, we will sooner or later have to reenter it.

Eventually, not turning away from our pain becomes a practice we've taken to heart. We no longer turn away from our turning away—this being akin to the capacity to be comfortable with our discomfort. In such uncommon inclusion, we open ourselves to what truly matters, regardless of its painful dimensions, grateful for the capacity to work with difficult conditions, grateful to simply be here.

A New Relationship with Our Pain

Pain can be a real pain, and it can also be something altogether different—if rather than turning away from it we *meet* it. We turn toward our pain; we enter it; we get intimate with its qualities, going into it until we reach its core. These are the essential steps, available to us when we take a nonproblematic orientation to our pain. Over and over again, we emerge. Our pain may not be gone, but we now have a very different relationship with it—one that serves our healing and awakening. In being a deliberately conscious container for our pain, we become more capable of seeing what our pain contains.

Pain can be grace—perhaps a fiery or fierce grace, but grace nonetheless—if we don't allow it to become suffering. Pain hurts, sometimes terribly so, but we don't have to be victims of it; we may not be able to get rid of it or avoid it, but we can use it wisely. And after a certain point, what else is there to do?

Journeying to the core of our pain is more a trek into rugged terrain than a flatland hike, asking that we breathe courage into our stride, step by conscious step. The more deeply we commit to this journey, the less we resist or fight it, and the more grace-filled it tends to become. There's no glamorizing of pain here; going into it can be very difficult at times, but nonetheless can still be done.

Directly facing and getting to know our pain from the inside helps us make wise use of it—and eventually to find freedom *through* our pain. As we engage more and more fully in this process, we realize right to our marrow that our suffering is optional, even as we continue to live with the presence of pain in our lives.

Pain isn't blocking our path. It's part of our path.

The ongoing practice of meeting, naming, entering, and becoming intimate with our pain strengthens and illuminates our way, paving it with heart, guts, and vision.

Into the Place Where Our Pain No Longer Pains Us

When we reach the core of our pain, we discover that our pain is no longer just pain. Though it may still hurt, it doesn't hold sway over us. Its voice is no longer our voice. We're neither looking through its eyes nor fleeing it. We've stopped giving in to it, and we've also stopped fighting it.

We have, in short, taken much of the pain out of our pain. Put another way, our pain no longer pains us. It still may hurt, but we now experience it not as an obstacle but as an attention-deepening blend of phenomena that the word *pain* can't do justice to.

This is the fiercest sort of grace. The journey into and through our pain hasn't necessarily rid us of the unpleasant sensations of our pain, but it has significantly freed us from their gravitational imperatives, their tar-pit traps. Here we find freedom not from our pain but *through* our pain. We're simply present with our pain, using it to be more deeply anchored in what truly matters.

This isn't to advocate any sort of masochism or sticking with pain no matter how hellish it is. No teeth gritting, no grim-faced holding on, no stoic heroics—such stands mostly just reinforce the very ego-centricity (see what *I'm* putting myself through!) that, by treating our pain as an adversary, prevents any intimacy with it.

It's of central importance to realize that there's no need to always avoid pain-reducing medication. There's no inherent spiritual virtue in not taking such medication. If taking the edge off our pain allows us to journey more readily to its core, so be it.

Taking the pain out of our pain means claiming a solid seat in the midst of our discomfort and hurt, a seat firmly rooted in a deeper now. The dragon is now in the background or perhaps even gone to nothing, its energies now ours, both fueling and illuminating our steps.

We're now becoming grateful to the dragon, for its sheer presence forced us to go deeper, to call upon the very finest in us, to access unsuspected levels of courage. And the treasure it was guarding? It was, and is, none other than yet another aspect of our essential being, pervaded by a love and power that serves the fullest good of one and all. At first it was "my" treasure, then "our" treasure, and at last "the" treasure. What we had to go through in order to reach the treasure ensured that we would, upon reaching it, not be inclined to claim it as just "mine."

When pain is no longer just pain, we're not only on our way home but already in touch with the hearth.

PART FOUR
EXPLORING SHARED
SHADOW

31 GENERATIONAL TRAUMA AND COLLECTIVE PTSD IN OUR SHADOW

Generational Trauma

Our shadow not only contains what we don't want to see or feel in ourselves but also what we don't want to see or feel in the history of our predecessors. Some of the events of our past had enough impact to decisively alter our direction, to imprint us with certain behaviors, to emphatically condition us. This we know.

What we might not know, or know as well, is how we're impacted by events that happened not only before we were conceived but also before our parents and their parents were conceived—and back through historic and prehistoric times, back into the long shadow of the past before our past. The past and its defining events and forces haven't necessarily weakened with the passage of time. Such events, such forces, exist as fields of intergenerational presence and gene-tweaking influence. These fields—akin to but far more complex than magnetic fields—can't be seen but can be felt, intuited, registered by more than our everyday mind. Not being aware of these fields doesn't mean that we're immune to them. Just as another's mood, however subtle, can get beneath our skin, affecting and altering our state, so too can the force fields of our far history, rippling as they do not only through our consciousness but also through our very cells, significantly affecting our emotional and psychological structuring.

What shaped those who shaped us can't help but impact us from somewhere behind the scenes. Much of this impacting is housed in our shadow, in the form of impressions—mental and sensory, noticed and unnoticed.

We may recognize the role that our parents' and grandparents' unresolved wounds played in the formation of our conditioning but ignore or underestimate how we're affected by what conditioned them. This might seem abstract or intangible, but if you attune yourself to your parents and grandparents and the worlds in which they grew up—both in familial and cultural contexts—you'll likely sense a certain cultural atmosphere, and you'll become more aware of the mix of powerfully influential factors that created the multidimensional field in which they lived.

Think of parents and grandparents who came of age during America's Great Depression, especially those who were in dirt-poor families, barely eking out a living. They were uniquely shaped not only by their own parents' behavior but also by the prevailing atmosphere of the times. Even if they became wealthy in their adult years, they may have retained much of the mood of their earlier times, penny-pinching when there was no need to do so, acting as if the Great Depression was still lurking just outside their door. As their children or grandchildren, we may not have felt deprived or worried about finances, but the not-having-enough mood of their early history might still be seeping into us, indirectly affecting us in ways that aren't so much financial as emotional and relational, as when we hang on to things that we know we ought to let go of.

At least some of what constitutes such unnecessary retention is likely housed in our shadow, and the most elusive part of this at a feeling level is probably the cultural field of influence in which our parents and grandparents were raised. When we're being run by our shadow, not yet significantly recognizing it, we're also, in part, under the influence of that which was culturally implanted in our ancestors.

Let's take this a big step further: Imagine the major shocks and traumas that those who lived thousands of years ago had to endure, without the anesthetizing buffers and comforts we now have. We can romanticize those times, make costume dramas out of them, forgetting how incredibly difficult life was then. Life for almost all was packed with huge hardship—omnipresent slavery, massive famines, basically no human rights, and an average lifetime of less than half of what it is now. Great plagues, medical ignorance, serfdom, warfare, and everyday brutalities left unimaginable trauma for almost everyone in their wake (along with compensatory numbing and soul-crushing resignation). This trauma has been transmitted through the generations, unhealed and still festering. Not that life isn't still a hell of a challenge, but plenty of us—with obvious exceptions, such as those living in poverty, slavery, and war zones—have it much easier now, having a comfort that those from long ago could only dream of. Even the kings and queens of old in many ways had less comfort than those in middle-class America have now. And our ancestors didn't have the tools to work with and heal trauma; they simply carried it in their systems, transmitting it to their children. Trauma wasn't named as such but was instead normalized.

We have the imprint of our ancestors' history and traumas in us, lodged in our flesh, psyches, and shadowlands. It's encoded in us, branded into us far below our skin, awaiting our consciously embodied encounter with it. To really explore our shadow is to also explore our intergenerational shadow, and such exploration must be a more-than-intellectual journey. We need to get past our avoidance of not only our own traumatic past but also that of our ancestors. Avoiding or paying too little attention to such shared history leaves it free to control us, to infect and fester in us.

The big step that's needed is turning toward our personal and ancestral pain—in ways that don't further traumatize us—and connecting the dots between our past and present not just mentally but also emotionally, psychologically, and spiritually. Without thus facing our generational pain and entering it with wholehearted attention, we can't see it clearly enough to make the needed connections.

Turning toward our pain, including our ancestral pain, is difficult, messy, often chaotic—not something that can be advertised to the public as a wonderful thing. How do you market the need for us to leave, *really* leave, our comfort zones, exiting the cozy cave behind our forehead for the wilderness of our guts and heart-wounds and shadow? The answer is, you don't market it; you *do* it, without fanfare or applause. The odds of a majority of people seeking to address not only their personal pain but also the pain they're carrying forward from their ancestors are very, very low. But as more individuals make a start, one or a few at a time, beginning by bringing their shadow out of the dark, a shift on a larger scale will get seeded.

Collective Post-Traumatic Stress Disorder (PTSD)

Post-traumatic stress disorder (PTSD) is the name clinically given to a mix of symptoms following a traumatic event or arising during a period of trauma. These symptoms may surface right away, or they may take some time to surface. In severe cases, they are unusually upsetting and darkly overwhelming, generating a sense of deep disorientation—a destabilization that leaves us on distressingly shaky ground and our sense of self in bewildering and often frightening disarray.

The levels of PTSD range from severe to moderate to mild, in both personal and collective contexts. PTSD gets mainstream consideration these days, and various treatments are offered that range from the pharmaceutical to the conventionally therapeutic (usually overly cognitive) to, all too infrequently, the deeply therapeutic. In psychological literature, there's a relatively clear demarcation between those with PTSD and those without it.

PTSD is a modern label, but what it stands for has been around for a very long time. Given the often brutal conditions under which our ancestors lived, it's highly probable that they had PTSD—not just personally but also collectively. In most societies throughout history, pretty much everyone except for the wealthiest had zero privileges. For most people, daily living was filled with do-or-die harshness, which included plagues, famines, very high mortality rates, and brutal disregard for human rights, plus the emotional dulling needed to endure such conditions.

This collective PTSD has been transmitted—biochemically, emotionally, and psychologically—from generation to generation, with little or no awareness that this has happened. It occupies much of our shadow, both personally and collectively. It's possible that all of us carry the echoes of PTSD, to however slight a degree. And it's also possible that our species itself is suffering from PTSD. Just because the symptoms of PTSD may not seem to exist in some of us doesn't mean that they aren't there—after all, we're capable of considerable repression. However well-adjusted we may be or may seem to be, is there not some residual shock, however faraway or muted, in us and our history—at least some core anxiety, some sense of impending disaster, some numbness, some sense of being driven by past events, some existential edginess, along with at least some sense of sharing all of this?

We may turn away from those with obvious PTSD symptoms, such as war veterans or survivors of childhood horrors, but in such aversion we're turning away from our own PTSD, our own core-level wounding, seeking ever more successful distraction from it and from the raw pain that animates it—as well as from the pain of those who are slammed by it. And though collective PTSD is subtler than the crippling PTSD that war veterans are often burdened by, it's insidious, gnawing its way through our interior.

When any condition persists long enough, we tend to normalize it. We adapt. The collective PTSD from which our species suffers has been normalized, accompanied by collective numbing and a dazzling wealth of potent distractions for those not living in poverty. PTSD isn't just a matter of overwhelmingly unpleasant recall and reaction but also of the "solutions" to this—namely those practices and things with the potential to distract us from our suffering. When low-grade PTSD and its "solutions" are normalized, and their bare reality tucked away in our shadow, we become significantly numb or nonresponsive to even the most serious of situations.

For example, the fact that we possess the capacity to annihilate our species—the potential for full-out nuclear war hasn't stopped lurking—has become mostly just a background consideration, something to not really feel, despite its reality. Though it needs only certain people under certain conditions at the controls to make it happen, we tend to see our possible oblivion with something akin to the vacant stare of a junkie who has just shot up with much more than what they originally planned.

Much of our collective PTSD has slipped so deeply into our shadow that it seems nonexistent, except perhaps as dimly lit background moods that periodically get to us. But it remains—muted and not so easy to differentiate—still there. What's especially needed in the face of collective PTSD is, first, *de-numbing*, which begins with recognizing our numbness—and our habit of numbing ourselves to our numbing. Feeling into what's really going on beneath our numbness can be overwhelming at first, but with practice we can keep our capacity to feel set to a level that doesn't blow us away. De-numbing activates our compassion, potently reconnecting us to others, known and unknown, nearby and faraway, enlivening our sense of us-in-it-together no matter what the conditions are.

The next step to getting to our collective PTSD—to sense it more than just mentally—is for each of us to face and work with what's in our personal shadow, deeply and thoroughly. When we're well into this labor, we're able to turn up our intuitive radar for more distant signals, perhaps beginning with our felt sense of our parents' personal and collective influences, and then moving further back in time. Take it as far back as you can. Instead of just being entertained by depictions of cave-dwelling humans from long ago, feel into those beings and their ancestors; look through their eyes, sense their environment, their fear and care and love.

We're moving so, so fast now as a species, largely overcome by our accelerating culture, electronic environment, and rampant self-poisoning. Our deepest knowing is all but drowning in all the excess information, suffocating in the data smog that we take to be just the way things are. But there's another world so close by—one that's quieter, less rushed, much more alive and practical, connected to what's truly essential—bringing together past and present in ways that awaken and heal, allowing us to shed our shock and numbness. This other world, as always, remains available to us. It is, as always, home. Our work is to turn toward it, realigning ourselves with it without any abandonment of our wounding and basic humanity and responsibilities. Bit by bit. Now.

32 COLLECTIVE SHADOW UNVEILED

JUST AS EVERY INDIVIDUAL has a shadow, so too does every grouping of us, be that a family, tribe, company, religion, political party, or nation. This shared or collective shadow is ours to recognize and explore. To not know it is to keep ourselves in the dark, increasing the odds of humankind's self-destruction.

Shadow unseen and unacknowledged keeps us divided, fragmented, mired in toxic us-versus-them dynamics.

Shadow elements that aren't seen as such are inevitably projected onto others. If my tribe has a distasteful quality, it may project it onto your tribe, while at the same time denying that it has this quality. Your tribe may or may not actually possess this quality, but my tribe is dead certain that you do, and it has no interest in investigating such certainty, regardless of some pesky facts that ought to make my tribe reconsider how it's viewing your tribe. (And if your tribe does indeed possess this quality and mine doesn't, my tribe still needs to recognize that we possess the *ingredients* of this quality.) It's no big surprise that my tribe's empathy for your tribe is very likely tucked away in my tribe's shadow.

Projecting our tribe's unsavory qualities onto others allows us to externalize our own collective shadow and relate to it as though it's not part of us but of *them*. Perhaps these others constitute a different race or nation; perhaps they have a different orientation politically, spiritually, sexually; perhaps they're alien to us. Whomever they are, turning others into a walled-off *them* is an all-too-common, far-from-empathetic action, featuring dehumanization and seemingly justified violation. Once we've reduced others to something less than human, hardening our heart against them, we can legitimize treating them badly: attacking, colonizing, and "cleansing" ourselves of them. This shadow-driven mind-set is central to the collective madness of war, which continues unabated in our times, just as barbaric and ugly as ever, regardless of our advances.

When we're caught up in collective shadow, we're dangerously out of touch, however convincingly we can rationalize what we're doing. We organize and arm ourselves in righteous reaction to perceived others whom we've unknowingly saddled with our own shadow.

This dense dualism, entrenched in unexamined certainties, plagues our species and has brought us to a very dangerous planetwide edge. This doesn't mean that dualism itself is a problem and that nondualism is a higher good, but that our differences need to be resolutely held in a space of mutual respect and care. And this isn't possible without knowing our shadow, both personally and collectively.

America the Not So Beautiful: The Shadow of the United States

In the early 1970s I traveled on the cheap for a year across Asia, mostly off the beaten track, getting to know people everywhere I went. One thing that was consistently shared with me was a strong aversion to the United States, especially with regard to its meddling in other countries' affairs. I was in Iran while the Shah was in power. The Iranians I met were outraged that his dictatorial violence was supported by the United States, and they would have probably treated me much worse if they suspected that I was American. I learned in those long-ago travels to ensure that my new acquaintances in each country knew I was Canadian, with a Canadian flag sewn prominently onto my backpack.

America's tarnished international image reached a new low with the election of Donald Trump and the continued voting-in of the Republican Party, despite its far-from-humane agendas and troglodyte mentality. Trump's slogan "Make America Great Again" presumes a past greatness that's but a fantasy for a privileged minority. The "Land of the Free" has never been the land of the free. The United States has never really been united; there are and always have been deep fault lines running through America, cracks that make for a divided, at-war-with-itself country. What we're appalled by now in America has been central to it for a long, long time, solidly lodged in its considerable and largely overlooked shadow.

So what's in America's shadow, whether partially or fully? (As you read through the following list, remember that every nation has its own shadow.)

Shame. The more we push our shame into our shadow, the more aggressive and pride-bloated we tend to become. This is also true of nations, especially those that appear to be too big to fail. The powers governing America are, with very few exceptions, not grown up enough to express genuine remorse; truly losing face is anathema to them. When faced with past violations, it's much easier to get righteously aggressive, putting the heat on others. The degree to which America flees its shame is the degree to which it endangers the world, including its own citizens.

Fear. The American psyche is riddled with fear. This shows up not just as heightened everyday anxiety but also as normalized paranoia, a widespread affinity for conspiracy theories, an unquestioned pull to the "security" of fundamentalism, an excessive attachment to weaponry, and an exaggerated aversion to "outsiders" (not just foreigners but also non-Caucasian immigrants, blacks, socialists, non-Christians, and, ironically, Native Americans). Building bigger walls won't help cut through such fearfulness, nor will finding better tranquilizers, nor will being armed to the teeth. Until a significant number of Americans face their fear (both personal and collective) and get to the root of it, the "Home of the Brave" will continue to be a fear-driven land.

Narcissism and the unchecked egocentricity of American exceptionalism. Does any other country put as much energy into proclaiming that it's the greatest nation on earth? Rampant self-promotion and excessive flag-waving signal a toxically me-centered mentality. The recognition of this narcissism can't help but generate shame. If such shame isn't turned into aggression or otherwise fled from, a truly healing *humbling* can take place, cutting through the inflated pride that holds America as being better and more evolved than it actually is.

Bullying self-interest. The America-first mentality, carried to the profitable extreme, costs far more than humankind can afford. Disregard for and belittling of what's not aligned with American corporate and political agendas continues. Opposing these agendas often gets framed as a lack of patriotism.

An exaggerated need for self-protection. On a national level, unaddressed fear shows up in overbudgeting for defense and the global stationing of troops to make the world "safe for America." On the local level, feeling unsafe—fearful—is understandably very strong, given the high degree of violence in American culture, including mass shootings (now occurring at a rate of close to one per day). Part of the overpromoted "solution" to this is having one's own weapons. But this has simply *increased* fearfulness, making things even less safe. Fear has made for more guns, and more guns has made for more fear. Having easy access to guns doesn't necessarily make one feel safer, in part because such access means that more people who are dangerous or who don't like you will also have a similar access to guns.

Whitewashing of racist history. From its very beginning, the United States has been a land rigidly divvied up into haves and have-nots, featuring the dehumanization of the non-Caucasian latter. The fact that the founding fathers were slaveholders (as was the creator of the national anthem), even as they spoke in apparent sincerity about freedom and equality, still isn't given truly deep consideration in most circles of influence. Yes, other countries also practiced slavery, but few took—and take—such a grandiose stand as the United States in whitewashing, marginalizing, and denying their entrenched racism, allowing the racist streak in America to continue to thrive.

Attachment to being viewed as good, humane, the caretaker of the world. Many still view America as the bastion of democracy, goodness, and freedom, blinding themselves to the evidence to the contrary. America's self-interest commonly masquerades as altruism and care for others (in stark contrast to the genuinely altruistic activity of many US citizens).

Dishonor. The breaking of over five hundred treaties made with Native American tribes and genocide of many of those same tribes, the war in Vietnam, the weapons of mass destruction fiasco in Iraq, alliances with dictatorships, imperialistic ambitions masquerading as "nation building," interference with other countries' internal workings for less-than-noble ends—all of these are examples of dishonor in the extreme, dishonor that's still being denied or minimized in many circles of influence. The shame over such dishonor lies deep in America's shadow, finding outward expression mostly through an aggressiveness and myopic self-inflation that obscures any sign of actual shame.

Stunted morality. The Puritan ethic that colonized—and polluted—America from the very beginning is still very much alive, especially in the Republican Party.

Lack of empathy for its less privileged citizens. This is exemplified by not providing guaranteed health care for all Americans. Another example is demeaningly referring to social welfare programs as "entitlements," fueled by the chronic suspicion that low-income, poorly paid Americans are receiving "government handouts" undeservedly.

Misogyny. Still here, after all these years, still thriving, and still being denied or minimized by all too many. Yes, this is a worldwide phenomenon, but America tends to present itself as being better than other countries when it comes to treating women well—and uses this to camouflage or marginalize its own misogyny. Women in the United States are more often than not treated as second-class citizens, regardless of their status. Not until 1993 did marital rape become a crime in all fifty states. Sexual harassment of females in America is still viewed, to whatever degree, as a man's right in many places. And the list goes on.

Attachment to viewing its two-party system as offering real choice. Democrats and Republicans are, with very few exceptions, on the same side of the aisle—the party-before-country side— despite rhetoric to the contrary.

Intolerance of dissent; abuse of whistle-blowers. To take but one example, Edward Snowden exposed something that most would agree truly needed to be exposed and is still condemned by the powers that be.

Ecological myopia. This is exemplified by the denial or trivialization of climate change. Many in the United States are still lost in the fantasy of infinite resources.

■

Collective shadow material is surfacing at an unprecedented rate at this time in US history. What's going on behind the scenes politically and economically is more prominently out front nowadays, with its corruption, lies, metastasizing self-interest, and ecological illiteracy right in our collective face. And isn't this a good thing?

Yes, but only partially yes. Unfortunately, such exposure often tends—after some initial outrage and fuss—to quickly get reduced to just more infotainment and fast food for fast-fading thought, more twittering smog and impotent debate, numbing rather than awakening all too many of us. Sure, lying isn't a good thing, but if there's enough of it, and enough insistent recontextualizing of it (that is, "I didn't lie; I misspoke"), it easily gets normalized. It's just something that politicians and corporate heavies naturally do, right? The bar for real integrity has been lowered so much that it's all but buried.

America's shadow is surfacing, but this isn't making enough of a difference to really shake up the ruling dynamics of the United States. The impact of this surfacing periodically has a brief peaking, trending high on social media, but it's quickly dulled and flattened by being presented, however inadvertently, as something no more newsworthy than anything else having its headline moments, its viral flickers of fame. We're collectively bombarded and swamped by news, story after story on topics large and small, with the truly important and the trivial jammed into such close proximity that we all too often don't really register the difference, except intellectually.

This unhealthy leveling of distinctions is aided by omnipresent, high-impact distractions, including in-your-face reminders to keep on consuming—and not just news, but fast food, the latest gossip, porn, alcohol, and myriad forms of electronic sedation (including smartphone addiction). Also, think of all the commercial breaks, the relentless product placement, the ubiquitous sexy-as-possible advertising, the trivial updates that continually *interrupt* us—chopping up our attention span, diluting our ability to concentrate on things that really matter.

So we're both (1) witnessing more of America's shadow and (2) with too few exceptions, not allowing such witnessing to sufficiently impact us. There's so much in American culture to distract us (to whatever degree) from fully feeling and staying focused on the uglier truths of what's happening, so that the country's collective shadow gets far too little sustained attention.

The Civil War is still happening, and it's far from civil. There's a deep split down the very center of America, a jagged fault line that's *widening*, made more and more visible due to the exposure made possible through the mediums of electronic omnipresence and immediacy. On one side are the wealthy, on the other the rest of us. On one side are the Democrats and Republicans, providing a choice between right-wing and extreme right-wing policy; on the other side is everyone else, not yet aligned with a truly viable alternative but knowing that there's no point in staying put with the status quo and its waiting-to-be-broken promises and deep corruption. Put another way, on one side is unexplored shadow, and on the other side is the growing possibility of exploring—and making good use of—shadow, including collectively.

America's shadow can't be significantly unpacked by the powers that be because they have such a strongly concretized investment in their positions and prevailing views. Deep self-exploration is a no-no to them; very, very few American leaders openly undergo any psychotherapeutic exploration, let alone shadow work. Any who do risk being shamed for doing so, as if self-investigation—and truly knowing oneself—is a waste of time and a weakness.

Exposing and working with America's shadow is left to those who are working in depth with their own shadow. It's a minority, yes, but a minority that's starting to spread, with a core need of not losing depth as the practice widens. What's authentically good about America—its immigrant vigor, its resilience and pioneer spirit, its many altruistic and awakened citizens—will take deeper root and find more kindred company as America's shadow is brought out of the dark and subjected to fiercely compassionate exploration. Surely this is something worth investing in. Doing individual shadow work is the ground in which serious collective shadow work needs to be rooted. This kind of resolute individualism, inspired by real care for the greater good and a robust courage, is at the very heart of what's so sorely needed: *an awakened and truly responsible America.*

Working with Collective Shadow

When we're out of touch with our shared humanity, our shared suffering and yearnings and our shared grief, we're greatly diminished, and no amount of privilege and perks can truly compensate for the loss of our full humanity. Until we realize right to our marrow that what we do to others we do to ourselves, we're part of the problem—lost in the dramatics of our shared us-versus-them dreams, our collective hallucination.

Authentic shadow work cuts through such dramatics, awakening us to our conditioning both personally and collectively, helping bring everything—*everything!*—that we are into the circle of our being, consciously and fully. We don't just wake up but also mature, becoming truly responsible, staying connected to what really matters.

As we engage in this work, we become more aware of our collective fear, bringing it into the foreground of our consciousness. We sense not only the presence of this shared fearfulness but also its worldwide, darkly looming message: *We're threatened. We're not safe.* This insidiously broadcast anxiety eats into us, even as we find distraction from it wherever we can, including through collective amnesia and numb-ness. The collective us is in enormous pain, accompanied by enormous numbing. How else could we have brought ourselves to the brink of such planetary disaster and ecological insanity? Calls to just love each other, to be more humane to each other, to stop being so narcissistic, and so on, have basically no real impact, doing little or nothing to de-numb us. What's needed here is far less nice, far grittier, far more fitting: to turn—and continue turning—*toward* our pain, our aversion, our darkness; to get to know our shadow from the inside out and cease to let it control us.

Much of our work here is to *de-numb*. Yes, this means we now directly feel our collective fear, but we also can now more openly feel other collective states, ranging from outrage to grief, and know in our hearts that so many others, though very different from us, also feel these things. When we go to the core of collective fear, we sense others feeling such fear, suffering from it. Our hearts start to break open and our empathy kicks in. Our grief starts to surface—our grief over all the agony, horror, and pain endured by so, so many of us. Our grief then shifts from being personal grief only to *collective grief*—the grief of all of us, here and now, and through all history. This shared heart-hurt, along with the core-level, visceral recognition that we're all in the same boat, brings us all together, whatever our differences.

We can't afford to remain ignorant of our collective shadow. The peril of such ignorance is more than enormous. Shadow projection has always done damage, spawning war after war, but now the stakes are much, much higher, given our collective capacity to annihilate ourselves and commit ecological suicide. The destruction of our spe-cies and habitat is no longer a science-fictional fantasy but a looming reality, right in our collective face.

If we're to derail our rush to the cliff's edge, authentic shadow work is absolutely essential. Such work awakens us not so that we can rise above or transcend the mess we've made but so that we can clean it up, func-tioning skillfully from our core of being, holding humankind in our fiercely caring activist heart, putting our shared shoulder to the wheel.

In addition to knowing and working with our own shadow, here is what we can do about our collective shadow:

Recognize it. Implicit in this recognition is accessing enough self-reflection to see through the ways in which you've been entranced by your own conditioning, personally and culturally. When you start to see the reality of collective shadow, it's as if you're in a dream in which you know that you're dreaming; you're waking up even though the dream persists, and your awakening allows you to see what's happening in a new, much clearer light.

Turn toward it. This doesn't mean getting lost in our collective shadow and your reactions to it, but facing it with open eyes and heart, doing your best not to flinch from it. Yes, our collective shadow is enormous, but as you truly are, you are even bigger.

Get intimate with it. This begins with uncovering the ways in which you have participated in and colluded with collective shadow, and the ways in which you've been seduced and overshadowed by it. Instead of shaming yourself, you bring an increasingly compassionate eye to such past entrancement, making your way to its roots. Along the way, you explore the terrain carefully, feeling into what's beneath the surface, getting as close to it as possible without losing your focus.

Uncover your personal history with it. When did you first become aware of collective shadow? How long did you leave it unquestioned, and what were the consequences of questioning it? Are you still seducible by it, and if so, when? If there was trauma associated with it, have you faced this trauma and worked with it? When collective trauma is normalized, how can it best be challenged?

Name it, and keep naming it. Doing so creates just enough space for you to relate to collective shadow instead of being immersed in it. Naming our shared darkness is one of the first steps toward illuminating it.

Identify its predominant emotions. One of these is fear. Another, just as central, is shame, especially shame that's allowed to mutate into aggression.

Don't overlook collective trauma. It may seem to be absent when in fact it's buried deep or convincingly camouflaged by seemingly normal behavior. Identify it, feel into it, give it healing expression.

Explore collective fear. Become more attuned to its presence and messages (such as "we're threatened") without, however, allowing it to infect you. Note its impact on you. Don't numb yourself to it. When you go to its core and feel, really feel, how it's impacting others everywhere, you'll start shifting from fearfulness to a brokenhearted yet expansive compassion, step by conscious step.

Explore collective grief. There's so, so much grief everywhere, much of it mostly unexpressed, the bulk of it frozen in our shadow. So very many of us are submerged in unattended hurt and sorrow. Grief, fully felt and expressed, interconnects us all in profound ways. Sooner or later we shift from personal grief to shared grief to *the* grief, allowing our collective heartbreak and sense of loss to open us more fully to what truly matters. This brings a much-needed compassion to the exploration of collective shadow.

Cultivate a presence that can hold the pain of collective shadow. Such presence is the spirit of a full-blooded alignment of head, heart, and guts. It's courage, compassion, and integrity functioning as one. Its heart has room for all.

Cut through any tendency to dehumanize others. As much as you don't like the behavior of those under the spell of collective shadow, don't completely cast them out of your heart, including when you're taking strong stands against what they're doing. We're all in this together, whether sleeping or awake, numb or feeling, out of touch or in touch, lost or found.

■

The stakes have never been higher, but the opportunity to reach new depths of understanding, compassion, and humanity has never been greater.

CODA

DARKNESS UNVEILED

Turn, turn toward
What you're housing
In the dark
Meet it, uncover it
Until you realize
That what you're seeing
Is none other than you
In endarkened disguise

No longer blinded by light
You start unwrapping the night
Touching a knowing
Too deep to be spoken
A recognition
Too central to be broken
Until even the darkest day
Lights your way

ACKNOWLEDGMENTS

WRITING THIS BOOK was one hell of a labor of love.

When my energy for it waned and my psychospiritual work demanded my time, my wife, Diane, infused me with her deep care and vision, giving me both healing rest and the boost to freshly reenter my writer's cave. She also read, carefully, everything that went into the book, doing plenty of needed pruning, which was initially (not surprisingly) met with my resistance. I made case after case for my articulate blooms and my poetic excesses, but soon yielded to her insight gratefully. Having cofacilitated with me for ten years, she knows my work well! She did a lot of editing, helping me greatly to make this book more accessible to many.

My Sounds True editor, Amy Rost, did an exceptional job of shaping the book into something much clearer and more readable than I could have done on my own. Amy's skill in organizing my often-unkempt writing into user-friendly material was masterful. I could not have asked for a better editor.

And my gratitude to all those who have trusted me with the exploration of their shadow and deepest wounding. My time with you made this book possible.

ABOUT THE AUTHOR

ROBERT AUGUSTUS MASTERS, PHD, is a pioneering integral psychotherapist and group leader, relationship expert, and psychospiritual guide and trainer, with a doctorate in psychology. He's also the author of many books—including *Transformation Through Intimacy, Spiritual Bypassing, Emotional Intimacy,* and *To Be a Man*—and the audio program *Knowing Your Shadow.*

His intuitive, uniquely integrative work, developed over the past four decades, blends the psychological and physical with the emotional and spiritual, emphasizing full-blooded embodiment and awakening, emotional authenticity and literacy, deep shadow work, and the development of relational maturity.

At essence, his work is about becoming more intimate with *all* that we are, in the service of the deepest possible healing, awakening, and integration. He lives with his wife, Diane, in Ashland, Oregon. His website is robertmasters.com.

ABOUT SOUNDS TRUE

SOUNDS TRUE is a multimedia publisher whose mission is to inspire and support personal transformation and spiritual awakening. Founded in 1985 and located in Boulder, Colorado, we work with many of the leading spiritual teachers, thinkers, healers, and visionary artists of our time. We strive with every title to preserve the essential "living wisdom" of the author or artist. It is our goal to create products that not only provide information to a reader or listener, but that also embody the quality of a wisdom transmission.

For those seeking genuine transformation, Sounds True is your trusted partner. At SoundsTrue.com you will find a wealth of free resources to support your journey, including exclusive weekly audio interviews, free downloads, interactive learning tools, and other special savings on all our titles.

To learn more, please visit SoundsTrue.com/freegifts or call us toll-free at 800.333.9185.

SOUNDS TRUE
many voices, one journey